THE HAND

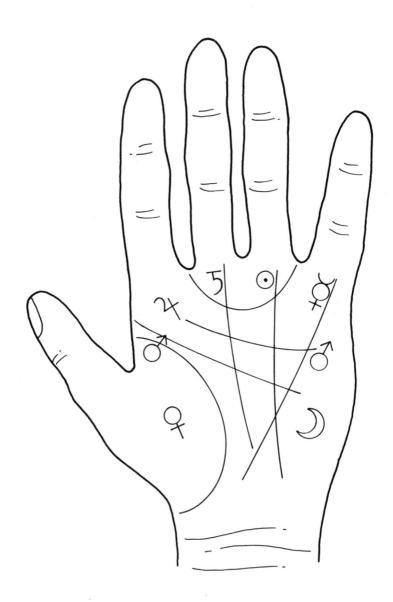

THE HAND

A SCIENTIFIC TREATISE ON PALMISTRY

A. RAPHAEL

**TYNRON PRESS
SCOTLAND**

Faithfully Yours
Raphael

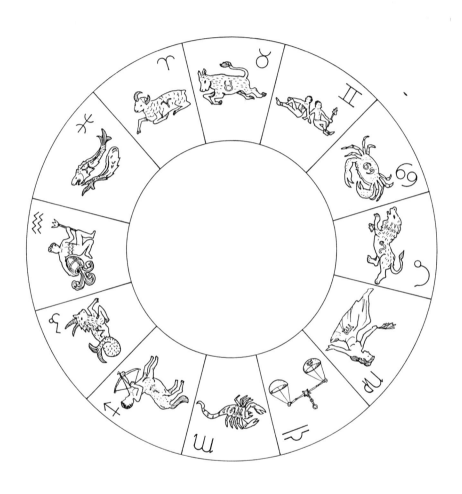

© *Revised edition, Tynron Press, 1990*

First published in 1901
This slightly revised edition first published in 1990 by
Tynron Press
Stenhouse
Thornhill
Dumfriesshire DG3 4LD
Scotland

ISBN 1-871948-44-4

Cover by Beatrice Ling
Printed in Singapore by General Printing Services Pte Ltd

PROLOGUE.

" There is a power that works within
us without consulting us."—*Voltaire*.

The author has had many years' experience with successful practice, being patronized by the aristocracy of
England, with the appreciation of the general public in the
leading cities of Europe and America; including London,
Liverpool, Manchester, Leeds, Antwerp, Brussels, New
York, Atlantic City and the West Indies, etc. His visits
to the above mentioned cities and countries have been the
occasion and the esteemed pleasure of reading many distinguished ladies and gentlemen.

His endeavors have been in the direction of a praise-
worthy effort to raise this eminent science to its proper
level, and place it above the so-called fortune telling, while
setting forth the true method of scientific delineations of
the Human Hand. With the researches of Voltaire, Dar-
win and other great writers as a basis, he presents herewith
an outline of his own system of hand-reading. The system is founded on the scientific fact, that each mental
faculty of the brain, in conjunction with the planets, exerts
a direct influence on the hand through the action of nervous or mental energy. Scientists have proven that there
are more nerve fibres and nerve cells connecting the palm
and the brain than any other portion of the body.

This original and descriptive method consists first, in furnishing an accurate description of the mental temperament, or disposition; second, a complete analysis of each line and mark, showing cause and cure for abnormal developments, with skill that seems uncanny.

This subject may be viewed from a natural light and will be found natural, and scrutinized from a religious standpoint will be found religious; good can be done through it, not only by its doctrines of the responsibility of life, but in its warnings, and in the knowledge of self it gives to all.

Should we discard it because opposed? No, rather help it, for the sake of truth that it possesses; use it because of its use, and teach it to others that its knowledge may be a power.

TABLE OF CONTENTS.

CHEIROSOPHY, (THE HAND).

PART I.

CHEIROGNOMY.

x CONTENTS.

PART II.
CHEIROMANCY.

CONTENTS. xi

LIST OF ILLUSTRATIONS

Diagram No. 4.

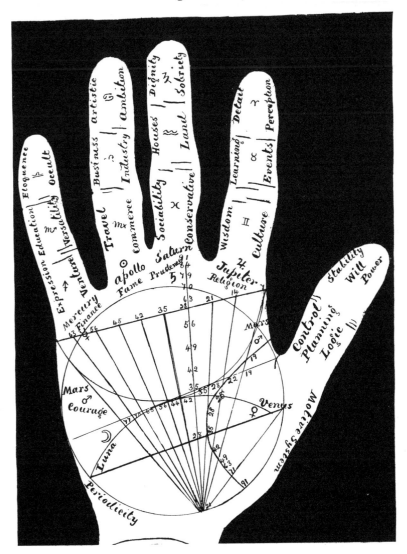

PREFACE.

Cheirosophy or Palmistry has arrived at the stage where it is now admitted as a Science—and a Science indeed it is, for no person can become a successful Palmist without a good knowledge and a keen understanding.

All Palmists have been working under difficulties for many years on account of inexperienced practitioners, gypsies and uneducated people, so-called Palmists. However we have now arrived at a successful stage, and outspread to a great extent those disreputable people and characters this peculiar work has had to contend with, and we cannot ignore the fact that all of us more or less have suffered, but it is now a thing of the past. Palmistry has gained a substantial footing, and it is being developed more and more every year and in harmony with other sciences, especially astrology, from which it takes its origin, for we have traced its mysteries to the stars, their influence on the earth and its denizens, and the magnetic fluid from their far-away splendor.

The author expects to see the day when he will publish his original work on the foot in conjunction with the hand, which will open out many valuable discoveries.

The Student should not attempt to give verbal readings until he has gained a thorough understanding of the science, which requires at least four of five months' study and practice with drawing. The first object to be taken is the shape of the hand on the whole, for it may be wide, narrow, long, short, flabby, hard, moist or dry, also thrown back or curved forward.   No one sign of itself should be taken without the corroborative evidence of others, and it is far better for the beginner to commence by taking impressions of the hands, marking round the finger and noting the size of mounts, etc., after which, when alone, carefully write out the delineations, having this efficient work for reference.   Then comes the consolation of an acquired science and a successful Palmist.   At the end of the book the reader will find an interesting article on Mysterious Phenomena, which were considered by the people of olden times to certainly exist.   This I do not guarantee.   Never-the less, it will be found amusing and interesting.   The student must judge for himself as to the truth thereof.

Diagram No. 5.

The Three Fates.

ASTROLOGY IN THE HAND.

Planetary influence is known to us and twelve individual rulers of the twelve zodiacal signs, and out of these twelve have been ascertained the sacred seven to whom have been given authority over the rest, and they are memorized by the days of the week, and represented by the palm and fingers of the right hand and by the left palm. The first four signs are represented in the right hand of the personality, the next four or complex signs in the left hand of the individuality. The first two of the remainder are in the right, and the latter two in the left. The sacred seven are represented in the hands by the five fingers of the left, and the forefinger and middle finger of the right hand. The process of the growth and birth of the Physical planetary system by the shrinkage and cooling of the Solar Mars in space rings, has been gradually thrown off by the sun. Therefore the third finger is the wedding-ring finger, the finger of the sun, which may on the right hand be defined as patience, devotion and thought; on the left hand the corresponding significations are faith, hope and love, which reminds us of St. Paul's words: "Now abideth faith, hope and love; but the greatest of these is love." The esoteric rulers of the days of the week are as follows: The Queen of Heaven—Hera, the ruler of Libra Love (left forefinger), who typifies the Sabbath; the Virgin of the World—Demeter, or Isis, left middle finger, who typifies Monday; the queenly Pallas Athena—the left thumb, who has gained the victory over death, typifies Tuesday; Hermis, the winged messenger, is typified by the left little finger and stands for Wednesday. Zeus retains his lordship over Thursday. Aphrodite rules over Friday, typified by the ring finger, and thus the celestial week is divided up into parts.

CHEIROSOPHY.

(THE HAND.)

The hand of man has glorified the earth with works
of science, art and industry, which are divided into two
branches—Cheirognomy and Cheiromancy. The vital
impress of all this has made the hand a faithful index of life
and character, foretelling incidents, accidents and liabili-
ties that endanger the progress of man; it reveals liability
to disease and organic prognosis, etc., as well as affording
much pleasure and interest. The twin sciences, Cheirognomy and Cheiromancy, are the means by which the past,
the present and the future may be read in the formation
of the hands. The shape of the hand, formed by the
bones and muscles, indicate the more solid elements—the
traits and framework of our character. The lines of the
Palm are termed Cheiromancy. The curves, spots and
stars show the changing events, which make up the course
of the individual. The natural uses of each part of the
hand determine what that part must signify in the art of
Palmistry or Cheirosophy.

Right and Left Hand—"Length of days are in her
right hand; riches and honor in left." Prov. Chap. III.
16 v.

The brain being a mental mechanism gives a decisive
answer to the character of the signs, respecting the posi-

tive and passive. The left side of the brain-lobe in a right-handed person is the more positive and larger side. The larger hand therefore acts as the positive hand, the executive and guiding hand—what the person would be of his own free will—the directive, impulsive elements of the individual.

The left hand is passive and receptive, calm, somewhat representing part destiny or hereditary endowments of parents, showing what the person would be if he yielded to the influence of others.

When, however, the right hand is passive and receptive, exactly the reverse is true.

The receptive hand is the hand of futurity or hereditary endowments; the right the positive and the hand of futurity by will-force.

PART I.

CHEIROGNOMY.

The Seven Types of Hands and Their Classifications.

They are determined as follows:

CHEIROGNOMY.

Form and Shape of Hand.—Size, Form and Texture of Thumb and Fingers.

THE ORDINARY OR ELEMENTARY HAND.

Indications—A hand coarse of texture, clumsy and hard; a large, thick, heavy palm, lacking in flexibility; short fingers and nails; generally a scarcity of lines.

Dictated to the Owner.

A low type of mentality may be allotted to the possessor of this hand. Your destructive propensities are prominent and active, your ardent passions require a great determination in exercising much restraint, to enable you to overcome those excessive affections which have been endowed to you.

The muscular part of your system is exceedingly strong, and your activity is great; mental capacity somewhat deficient. Roughly speaking, savages are found to be the owners of this particular hand. The artistic and spiritual world does not appeal to your nature, yet you may fear death. Neither do beauty, form and flowers interest you, and there is but little desire for culture, refinement or advancement for the benefit and intellectual growth of man. If you are the possessor of a short thick thumb,

Diagram No. 7.

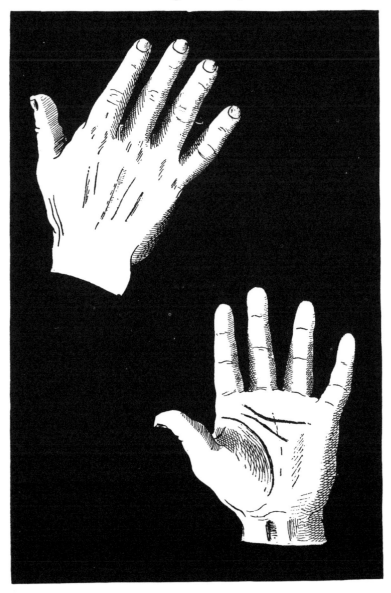

The Ordinary or Elementary Hand.

with a club-like heavy first phalange, you could become very violent in temper; more passionate and less courageous, with a cunningness which certainly is considered low, for instinct dominates reason.

The indications are that you can be influenced either for good or for bad by your associates and friends; you are not depraved at heart. Your sphere of life may be termed manual labor, agricultural pursuits, management of horses, cattle, navies, etc. The routine of work which may be rough and coarse, or that which may be carried out by the dim flickerings of the light of instinct. Science, office work and indoor confinement are not in your line. You are among the individuals that may be classed superstitious, especially if you are the owner of pointed fingers; phantoms and specters may trouble you.

The elementary hand endows you with heavy and sluggish feelings. The imagination appears asleep or needing an inert soul, lacking in enthusiasm. The thought of pain does not make you shudder, and you are not sensitive to the touch, your nerves being stronger than the higher and more developed type of humanity; but, nevertheless, you would soon succumb to pain, sorrow or bereavement, when it seriously sets in. At such times you will lack moral courage and be found wanting in resources.

This type of hand is not the expressor of purity, and is rarely found otherwise, unless in the polar latitudes. Your talents are few, and you lack the ability to invent or originate, being governed by custom and habit; you seek not to associate with energetic mentalities. Debate and reasoning is not looked upon as a necessity for existence; you are unlike the gallant soldiers who fight for their king and country; when you fight it is to defend yourself, not for glory and honor. Religion is not entertained as a necessity for your happiness. You have an ear which appreciates the strains of music; if you are a player, it will be from the ear rather than from notes.

Among the civilized races education to a great measure is annihilating or stamping out this class of hand, and modified types are often observed.

Your temperament is phlegmatic and emotionless; your will should practice the ascendency over the animal instincts and desires. Brutality should be avoided; do not too frequently indulge in drink or the pleasures of the earth. It is said that the subjects of this hand eat, drink, sleep and die. Distinguish yourself from the brute creation; save your money and contribute to the education of your children; reserve for a rainy day, and do not forget your Creator, for there is another life to come.

Diagram No. 8.

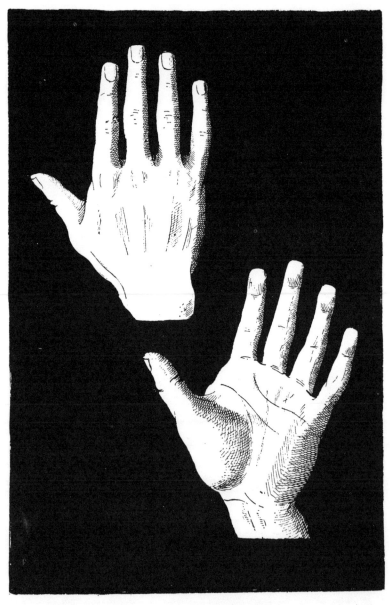

The Square or Useful Hand.

THE SQUARE OR USEFUL HAND.

Indications—Practically speaking square on all sides; usually inclines to size and noticeable in the width of the hand; square at the wrist and indeed, the whole aspect of the palm and fingers appears square.

DICTATED TO THE OWNER.

Your characteristics, which accompany this methodical hand of accuracy, especially if knotted, may be termed preciseness in manner, punctuality, order, classification and regularity of system. You are endowed with strong emotions, intense affections, which are not so demonstrative or gushing as found in the generality of people, owners of other classes of hands.

If your hand is found knotted, i. e., with developed joints, this adds greatly to the power and strength of character. The fingers have four distinct sides, more remarkable when compared with the round, conic finger. The finger nails are generally short and square at the tips.

Should you be the owner of smooth fingers, i. e., with undeveloped joints, you will be reasonable, respectful and obedient to those in authority, a lover of art and literature, possessing superior power for organization, with an outward appearance of indifference and coldness.

If knotted, among your characteristics will be found thoughtfulnesss, faithfulness, a law-abiding character, respecting authority and a lover of discipline, prudent and careful in business matters, a good mathematician, and would make a severe but unprejudiced judge. Yours may be classed among the hands of harmony and progress.

Never rash in promises, a true friend and staunch; possessing severe morality; a native intolerant of independent ideas or doctrines. Little enthusiasm is indicated, for you hold yourself well under control. Consider yourself an excellent detailist and fond of minutiae, especially if the fingers are long. Your honesty in business matters is to be relied upon, for you possess strong principles. You are often misunderstood in your immediate home circle, being cool and calm in affection, often looked upon as unloving; you will be found attentive to the duties of home, carefully providing the wherewithal. You are not enthusiastic over art, neither can you be called poetical, yet very determined when opposed, but adverse to quarrels. Instinct is soon counterbalanced by reason. You possess great perseverance and foresight as to how things may terminate. You demand a great amount from yourself, consequently are exacting with other people, expecting more sometimes than the lesser endowed mortals are able to give.

When this hand is found with a very long thumb, the individuals are very hard masters. You, being the possessor of the square hand, will abhor flattery, but appreciate commendation. It would be torture for you to be compelled to kiss and caress your relatives through courtesy, for you know when you are appreciated, and that is sufficient. You love truth and your element is with practical and useful things, seeking and obtaining substance, in preference to imagination and sham. The indications show you are not original, but prefer to walk in the beaten track with a fixed and determined purpose. In language forcible and simple, displaying depth of thought and strong reasoning powers; you prefer practical studies and exact sciences naturally. When carrying out your duties or when engaged in work you exercise great application, you love agriculture and favor commerce. You are a great disciplinarian and a slave to system and order; you comprehend things so far as you can deliberately see them, and do not, as a rule, jump rapidly at conclusions before weighing well the why and the wherefore, preferring common sense to genius, the useful to the beautiful, supporting the accepted order of things; a law-abiding citizen.

When the square hand is found, with short fingers, it will attribute to the subjects dominant faculties of rulership, practical and material in every sense of the term, and careful of own rights. These people are hard to persuade, being obstinate and narrow-minded. They acquire their wealth by hard work and careful savings; business-like but cannot be called speculators.

If you are the owner of the square hand with very long fingers, it denotes the intellect, stands pre-eminent and dominates the animal propensities, with strong inclination to formulate new plans and desire for investigations; you will be a great lover of detail and scientific research; not so prejudiced as the square with short fingers, for you proceed carefully and with caution, in order to arrive at reasonable decisions. You are somewhat tyrannical and faultfinding, especially if the knot of philosophy is found.

The natural position of the head line on the square hand is high, nearing the heart line, long and straight; the

sloping of the line towards the mount of moon is directly
opposite to the nature, and consequently the imaginations
would be cogent, and this would mean infinitely more than
one of greater slope on a conic or psychic hand.   Some of
our best painters, writers, and musicians have the square
hand with sloping head line; they commence their work
on a practical foundation, whether it be of the imaginative
order or otherwise, afterwards throwing in the imagination, whereas the conic or psychic will be found altogether
inspirational.

Diagram No. 9.

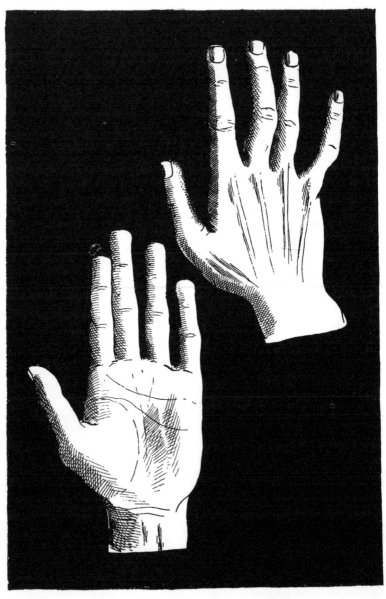

The Spatulate or Active Hand.

THE SPATULATE OR ACTIVE HAND.

Indications—The palm is wide, generally flat and thin, with large mounts, being broad the whole length; thumb large. The natural position of the head line, clear, long and sloping which adds to the characteristics.

DICTATED TO THE OWNER.

When your hand is hard and firm as above described, it signifies a restless nature, full of energy, of purpose and enthusiasm, with vivid nerve forces. If it be soft and flabby, a restless but irritable spirit is the result. You will have a tendency to display your abilities or work in fits and starts, being unable to stick to anything very long; change and diversity.

The owner of the spatulate hand, when firm and elastic, will possess power of invention and originality, with much independence.

Your characteristics are those of energy, intense love of action and freedom, with a marked combination of intuition, reason, dignity and defense, with intelligent foresight. Your hand belongs to inventors, engineers, discoverers, explorers and mechanics, possessing ability to penetrate untrodden fields of thought, often with plenty of self-confidence. There is an assertive right to possess a marked individuality of your own, in whatever grade of life you may strike out for yourself.

The individual possessing this class of hand is associated with and often becomes famous with inventions, and may be found in almost every walk of life.

Preachers with this formation are apt to be constantly

discussing the creeds they were educated in, yet they are precedent and undoubtedly the originators of our present day civilization.

As singers they are quickly individualized, and many of our best actors have spatulate fingers, likewise very expressive orators.

The indications are that the sense of independence inclines you to resent following other people's ideas, being as it were an advance agent of thought, desiring abundant means; a bare sufficiency not being enough.

If you own the spatulate hands with a broad development at the base of the finger, you will be remarkable for ability in the direction of an inventor of locomotives, ships and large pieces of machinery. Being very practical, you will direct your abilities and mind on the useful side of life.

It will be easily conceived that the thumb must be large to give the true character to the spatulate hand; the subject is resolute and self-confident, more active than delicate, more energetic than enthusiastic; in love will be more constant and faithful (though less tender and affectionate) than the conic or pointed-handed subjects, because the inclination for things romantic and poetic are lacking.

If you have spatulate finger tips, with smooth, i. e., undeveloped joints, you will love elegant and rich surroundings, also manifest a desire for such in the gratification of comfort; but it will be a fashionable rather than an artistic form of elegance. Looking for reality in art, being energetic in its pursuit, loving horses and dogs, science of agriculture and navigation; having talent for administration and command, as well as a capacity for the theory of warfare, and indeed, all enterprises where the mind directs the activity. Many with such hands are skilful musicians. Others make good colonialists, because they appreciate a country for what it yields to them and are not averse to manual labour, loving all forms of activity and hating a sedentary life. If their native land is poor or overcrowded, and the good things of life are scarce, they are quite satisfied to seek another country where there is promise of abundance.

The author concludes that this is the main reason for spatulate hands being so numerous in America. Of the hands he has examined in America and Canada, at least 70% have been modified or extreme forms of this type. The spatulate hand manifests admiration for architecture, but prefers the stupendous to the ornate. A city, to suit its tastes, must be well-planned, substantial, clean and business-like in its outlook.

Your spatulate hand loves to surmount difficulties and when it finds little to fight about, it may be inclined to practise almost any kind of sport - racing, jumping, shooting, etc. - to gratify the desire for activity and strife. It speaks forcibly and rules tyrannically.

SPECIAL TREATISE ON THE FINGERS.

A person possessing short nails which are twisted or ill-shaped, whose hands show but few lines, mainly those of head, heart and life, is of an unsympathetic, possibly even cruel and tyrannical disposition; sometimes of murderous instincts. If the finger of Jupiter is malformed and a low mount, the nature will also be inately selfish, mean, vulgar, with no self-respect or dignity of character.

If the possessor of such a hand is otherwise good, showing by numerous lines, the impressionability of the subject and the fingers are much twisted, such will indicate an aggravating, annoying disposition, given to mockery and petty deceit.

If you own fingers which have a tendency to turn back, being supple, this is indicative of a clever and sagacious person, affable, yet curious and inquisitive; much inclined to extravagance, which is generally indicative of mischief making.

When the fingers fit closely together, being thick at the third phalange, it shows selfishness and avarice; otherwise, that is with spaces so that when the hand is held up to the light, one can distinctly see through the chinks between the fingers, there are two meanings indicated according to the quality of the hands.

If the hands are well lined and a good mount of Jupiter, it will show a self-sacrificing and unselfish disposition; but if an unimpressionable hand, i. e., with few lines and any of the fingers illshaped, it will only indicate an inquisitive person. The twisted fingers should be considered from the reading previous.

If, when the hand is naturally opened, the first and second fingers are wide apart, this shows independence of thought; if the third and fourth are widest apart, independence of action.

Diagram No. 10.

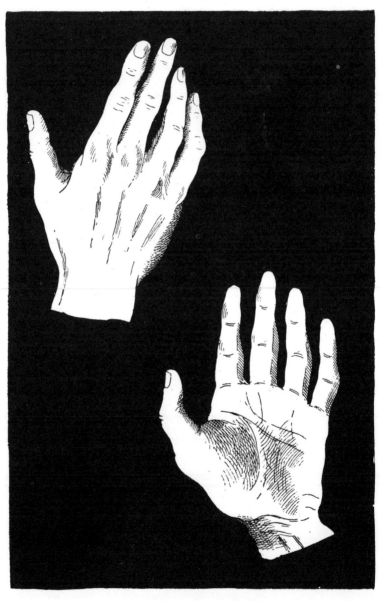

The Philosophic Hand.

THE PHILOSOPHIC HAND.

Indications—This type is known by its long, angular and bony fingers, tapering at the ends with enlarged joints, i. e., knot of philosophy or knot of order; rather long nails. Finger tips being of a conic formation. The appearance of the hand is ordinary but full of character. The thumb large, having the phalanges of will and logic about equal in length.

DICTATED TO THE OWNER.

Some cheirosophists divide these hands into two classes; one, that of the idealists whose ideas are derived from their inner consciousness. The other is where the ideas are envolved from external influence.

The owner of this hand may not be considered wealthy as regards the goods of this world; yet he may be rich in wisdom and knowledge.

You have the faculty of will power and logic well balanced; the phalanges of the thumb being equal in length, which illustrates evenness of determination, temper, reason and sense.

Your formation tends to mysticism, with capacity to enjoy the visions of imagination, construction and form. Consider yourself a student of human nature, or some peculiar subject, such as heathen mythology, history, biography, magic, etc. By nature you are meditative, very independent, fond of philosophy and deduction, persistent

in metaphysical studies, the faculty of calculation being
fully developed; a methodical individual, diligently seeking knowledge of abstract and absolute truth, delighting to
theorize and speculate practically with reality and custom.

The indications are that in all your works there seems
to be an absence of financial selfishness, yet you possess as
much ambition as most people, only of a different class.
Your one great desire is to individualize or distinguish
yourself from others, and for this purpose you will suffer
almost any kind of privation. You are very thoughtful
and earnest in the pursuit of wisdom and a lover of mystery
in every way.

Your philosophic hand loves detail and is careful over
small matters; having aptitude for minute and deep
thought, manifesting a quiet and secretive demeanor.
When injured you do not forget, but rarely if ever seek
vengeance; you seem to prefer to wait until an opportunity
presents itself, and in this you show great patience. Reason is your guiding principle. You doubtless are devoted
to religion, and very self-sacrificing in the defense of the
same.

The possessors of such hands should seek to avoid adverse introspection, and should aim at active, harmonious
pleasures, avoid magnifying trivial matters into mountains
of injustice; also the tendency towards negation should be
guarded against.

You are a lover of harmonious combinations, discord
and inharmony may disturb your digestive organs. Your
associates may term you proud or high-minded, but in
this direction not as others.

The head line is generally long and closely connected with the life line, which is set low on the hand. A variation of this, when set high upon the hand with a straight head line, the native manifests much energy in studying human nature, looking for wisdom, dissecting and criticizing associates, often exposing their weakness with ridicule, but with a genius that really discredits human philosophy.

THE CONIC HAND

OR HAND OF EXPRESSION.

Indications—This formation of the hand is generally found of a medium size, palm large and slightly tapering. The fingers are conelike in shape, being prominently full at the base; the tips of the fingers are not so pointed as the psychic.

DICTATED TO THE OWNER.

Your hand lacks the appearance of resistance and strength; yet indicative of instinct and impulse, with a love of beautiful things and ideas.

If your hand is large, very firm and the palm excessively developed, you will then be subject to excessive affections, which may lead to sensuality and desire of self-gratification. Under such circumstances the ties of domestic life may be unbearable, yet at heart you may be somewhat pure in many respects.

The possessor of the conic formation of the hand will be excitable, loving art and fiction, a novel reader, loving luxurious surroundings, and considerate (very) of your own comfort. Your patience requires development, for you tire too quickly. Your character tends towards changeableness and impractibility; you may be clever and quick in thought, showing fine intuition and foresight, but seldom carrying out plans. Pride is fully developed, which appears to its best advantage in company, and you have a love for praise.

Diagram No. 11.

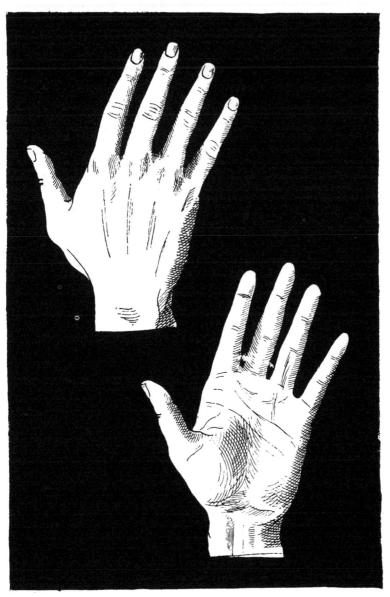

The Conic or Hand of Expression.

Your nature is quickly angered, and likewise easily pacified; you may be termed a good conversationalist, grasping the drift of a subject quickly, yet somewhat superficial, not really profound in knowledge or in any one special direction. You lack the power to concentrate your mind upon mental studies, therefore would not make a successful student. Your judgment is quick, guided by impulse, yet generous and kind, and when interested genial; rather changeable in friendship and affection, easily offended over small matters, carrying likes and dislikes too far. There is a tendency to be much influenced by surroundings and associates.

The indications show that you are too impetuous to consider words or expressions, but desire to demonstrate your talents at command, which results in brilliancy and accomplishments; often shining much better than anticipated, but lack the power to explain how the results are brought about. Your nature cannot be considered selfish as regards money matters, you being too easily persuaded to give, which is generally done on the impulse of the moment and without due consideration; consequently you often contribute where it is really not needed. A pitiful tale moves your emotions and sympathy, and you give away your substance before taking the trouble to consider the wisdom of the act.

Your temperament signifies that you cannot bear much pain or sorrow, soon sinking to the lowest depths of despair over small troubles; and then just as soon rising to the mountain top with delight and joy over a small pleasure. You are purely emotional, impulsive in thought and action, possessing artistic feeling, impressionable and excitable, lacking the ability of the money-maker, but visionary, poetic and romantic.

With reference to the head line. The natural position is sloping towards the Mount of Luna, or often arrives at the middle of that mount; when this is the case, there is an absolute leaning towards sentiment, romance and ideality, but a lack of practical methods. Whereas, when the conic hand is found with a straight head line, remarkable results follow. The subject will use all their artistic ideas and talents, but in a practical direction, apparently knowing by intuition and instinct exactly what is saleable or in public demand. Such individuals set to work and quickly produce some art of work, and as rapidly find a customer willing to purchase the same. The indications are they as a rule care less for the art than the money it brings.

Under these circumstances you will do six times as much work as the subject with a sloping head line; your common sense conquers the natural love of ease and luxury indicated by a sloping head line, where art is loved for its own sake, but in the case of a straight head line it is appreciated for the money it brings.

Diagram No. 12.

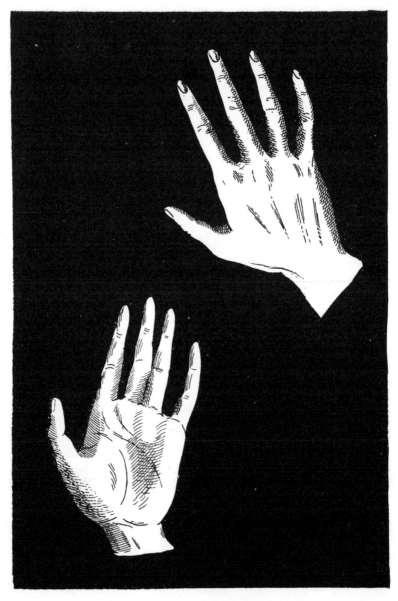

The Psychic Hand.

THE PSYCHIC HAND.

Indications—In form this hand is known by the large and slender-built frame, with pointed fingers. In health, has a very pale, pink tint and often a nicely shaped thumb. The hand is small and delicate.

DICTATED TO THE OWNER.

Yours is the hand that may be termed remarkable from a standpoint of beauty, but it cannot be classed with the useful hand, neither is it a practical one.

You manifest a desire for the love of poetry and art, but little energy is exercised in the execution of either; you possess the delicacy and pure instinct of art and nature. Lusts of the flesh and worldliness are not in your line, for you exercise your thought in the realm of the beautiful, and contemplate our celestial attitudes. You are easily disgusted by rough and coarse people; to live with the angels, comparatively speaking, is more to your desire. Really, you are unfitted to battle with this world, lacking force and energy, or ability to withstand temptation.

The present day break-neck race for gold holds no attraction for the possessor of the psychic hands; their ideas and aspirations soar far above this world and its dross to realms of beauty and spiritland.

You dream, imagine and fancy beautiful pictures, things that are visionary and impractical, consequently when thrown upon your own resources or compelled to face the world with all its hideous realities, are very liable to sink to the lowest depths, being unable to compete with the stronger formations in the struggle for the common necessities of life, and are liable to slide down the first easy path which invariably leads to destruction, without being conscious of the results.

You should seek for more realities, cultivating the real for the sham or imaginative; become more practical, for the borderland or unseen spiritual world is not yet at hand.

Your nature is dependant and you seek to associate with refined and noble mentalities. Your vital forces are delicate and weak. The faculty of imagination and ideality is fully developed.

You are liable to establish too lofty ideas and belong to the realm of prophecy, being full of electricity or magnetism. Should you direct your faculties in the direction of art you would paint subjects of wild romance and formulate symbols or pictures for imaginative representations. If highly developed, the soul is the first consideration; the treatment of material subjects of this world is really a secondary matter. Indeed, you are distinguished for your incomprehensibility.

This type, when excessive, produces the Oriental luxurious dreamer, devotees of physical phenomena, with a tendency to be a subject under imaginary spiritual influences.

THE MIXED OR COMBINATION HAND.

Indications—This is peculiar in itself, having no particular formation, viewing it on the whole; palm neither square, spatulate or conic. It may have a conic first or fourth finger, a square second and spatulate third; the thumb may be firm or supple long or short.

DICTATED TO THE OWNER.

The chief characteristics indicated in your hands are versatility with numerous ideas, changeableness of purpose, clever but eratic in the application of talents; your conversation is various and apparently brilliant in many directions, but perfect in none. If the head line be strong, you will choose and cultivate your best talents, and under such circumstances, may become proficient.

In practice I have observed that many with the mixed hands turn to the stage as a means of livelihood, but in this case the third finger is long and spatulate.

Individuals or the possessors of these hands are restless, and indeed, find in many cases success in changes and inventions, particularly in a direction of lighter labor.

You experience little difficulty in getting along with different dispositions, for you possess great adaptability to circumstances and the immediate requirements of the moment; you often may be found applying yourself to two or three different kinds of business, your knowledge being more superficial than profound in any one direction. As the saying runs, you are liable to have too many irons in the fire at once. You may play a little on several instru-

ments, sing a little, paint a little and be found very enter-
taining in company; your chief fault is you do not stick to
one thing long enough to become expert. Your mind is
always open to new ideas, and ready for anything that will
please and gratify the desire for change and variety.

The best direction to exert your talents, is to study
out what you are best adapted for, and settle upon such
with a determination to succeed; also discipline yourself
and hold fast to that which is good, discarding the minor
qualities, directing all forces and energy in one channel.
A responsibility might settle you, when you once overstep
the line of restlessness, you are capable of a mighty work.
Your associates may term you a jack of all trades, and
this is often true. You are subject to change your residence as well as occupation, and you should bear in mind
that a rolling stone gathers no moss. Your attributes
may be considered as versatility and changeability of purpose; you can readily adapt yourself to the custom of a new
country or fresh surroundings and easily make yourself at
home in whatever direction Fate may bring you.   You
possess a fair combination between the practical and imaginative, especially if the first half of the head line be
straight and the other sloping. Selfishness is fully developed, and you excel in scheming. You must not consider
yourself a good business man.

If your hand is a combination of the elementary and
psychic there are no indications of your rising or becoming prominent or really famous, your ideas being of too
great a variety to excel or become notorious.

CHARACTERISTICS AS INDICATED BY THE MOVEMENT AND ACTION OF THE HANDS.

The habitual actions of the hands are of great importance, and their natural positions should be considered. Every individual unconsciously demonstrates his inward emotions and characteristics more or less according to disposition and temperment.

An individual who carelessly throws about his hands, regardless of method or order, entirely lacking preciseness, making many changes, his members hanging carelessly and loosely at his side in the most convenient place, signifies laziness, restlessness and a suspicious character. When the hands are kept tightly closed, it denotes secretiveness; the same position when walking indicates a timid nature. The hands when naturally open, betray liberality and an open disposition.

A swinging of the hands to and fro while walking, tends to promptitude and impetuosity of nature. On the contrary, the hands kept motionless show a quieter and more dignified character with reserve. If the movements of the body and the hands are kept very precise, vanity and conceit often appear.

When the hands naturally fall towards, or appear contracted to the lower abdomen, sensuality prevails.

The body at rest and the fingers at work tapping or twisting, is indicative of a light, dreamy mind or fantasy, but when they beat together with energy and tremble, it signifies a highly nervous temperament.

Hands and fingers contracted towards the head indicate that part of the brain has a tendency to overwork, or else a weakness or pain. Deep thinkers and even schoolboys place their hands on the head when concentrating.

SHORT HANDS.

Short hands indicate a person impatient of detail, whose judgements come quickly, preferring to manage things on a large scale. If the fingers are pointed, imagination assists, but only the whole will be considered. Details tend to be ignored. Ideas and plans can be too large or grand to be practical. Handwriting usually large and bold.

LONG HANDS.

Long hands show capacity for detail, but if very large, liable to be over-meticulous. When the fingers are very long, the owner is active in mind and body, susceptible and emotional; if pointed, tact is indicated, and poetic tastes.

A person with a narrow palm and long fingers will be tyrannical and fault-finding.

The finest work, both mentally and physically, is done by people with large hands, but excessively large hands are intolerant. Coupled with square fingers, they indicate cruelty; and if knotted, they hint at mania.

LONG PALM.

If the palm is much longer than the fingers, the vital and animal nature predominates.

Such a person has little love of detail and is easily pleased. Contradiction, debate and contention are not in his nature.

The following rule may be followed: the lower part of base of the hand represents the physical; the upper part (i.e. the fingers) is indicative of the mind. If the palm and fingers are of equal length, the subject is even-tempered and usually shows good balance between judgment and instinct.

SMOOTH HANDS.

Smooth hands denote an impressionable nature, caprice and inspiration. With few lines, they show an even disposition or temper. These hands being generally soft, the fact of the matter is that they will not exert themselves to get out of temper, but, if their anger is aroused, they know the reason why.

Soft hands covered with a host of fine lines like a network are extremely sensitive, nervous and easily agitated, discomposed and worried by small matters. This nature imagines all sorts of ailments and troubles.

Some of my readers who have such hands may think their complaints are an exception, exclaiming, "But I really am sick; the fact is evident to others!" Possibly, this is so, but be mindful that most, if not all, diseases are from the mind, and imagination may be so wrought upon that the sickness is unto death: whereas if the will is asserted, recovery is a certainty and rapid progress the result.

Those with smooth firm hands are more successful with other people's affairs than their own. They are always upright, trustworthy and impressionable. If hard and rough to touch, the subject will be quarrelsome.

When the hand is covered naturally with a fine, light skin of a pink shade, the person will retain the bouyancy of youth.

When the hand is hard with few lines, the intellect is dull, such a person would find difficulty in learning; they are not susceptible but apathetic.

The palm, pale and almost white, the subject will take very little interest in anything outside himself, being selfish and unsympathetic.

When yellow in color, the nature is morbid and melancholy, sometimes morose.

When of a delicate pink, a sanguine, hopeful and bright disposition is indicated, helpful to self and others.

When very red, ardent in spirit, the temper quick, rather passionate, but of strong and robust health. Such individuals have the mounts of Mars predominant.

Hard hands show flagrant perseverance, and are generally reliable and steadfast in affections, yet in this direction not so demonstrative in home life, nevertheless sincere.

Excessively hard hands show no intelligence, and natural stupidity.

Soft hands show carelessness, idleness, indolence, with a tendency to sensuality; if thick and white with no noticeable change in color, whether warm or cold, this is a sure indication of absolute selfishness. These qualities may be applied to any hand which always appears white in any temperature.

The texture of the hand has nothing whatever to do with the skin becoming rough and hard by the kind of employment followed, but the consistency when pressed.

Some hands are soft and flabby. Some hard and inflexible. Others elastic and responsive; the latter are the best, as they give a character, earnestness, industry, faith and affection.

A hand hard and dry, appearing skinny, often indicates timidity, a nervous, worrying disposition; also poverty of intellect.

A very hollow palm is invariably a sign of failure respecting money matters, and generally the possessors of such experience more disappointments than real falls. If the hollowness tends towards the fate line, it foretells misfortune in money and business; when towards the head line, probably brain troubles, and when hollow about the heart line disappointments in love matters or affairs of the heart.

THE THUMB.

The thumb signifies the three great powers, love, logic and will. When the thumb is long and well shaped, that is, neither extremely stiff nor excessively supple and set low down on the hand, it will indicate force, active will power, reason and talent, harmony and blendableness, giving passive resistance and disposes of eccentricity.

If excessively long, when compared with the remaining part of the hand, it shows a very determined and tyrannical nature.

When very short and weak, the individual is too easily influenced for evil. Parents having children with this formation should impress them persistently with the importance of doing right; also watch them closely, for they are possessed with a feeling that to do as others do, whether right or wrong, is easiest and quite a thing of importance.

People with short thumbs make good servants and the best soldiers, doing well and being happier under control and discipline.

When medium in length, the subject will be passive as regards their desire for controlling others; but if the first and second phalanges be of equal length, this denotes a strong character with wisdom and good common sense.

The length of the phalanges relatively should be carefully taken into consideration, as a correct notification of these will assist the reader greatly in arriving at the general characteristics of his subject.

Diagram No. 13

Narrow Waist

FIRM Jointed

Supple

Logic &.
Lacking
Will Power.

The Thumb.

First phalange containing the nail, when longest, shows a very forcible will; the subject depends on neither reason nor logic, but upon will, therefore often causes himself needless trouble and annoyance.

If broad or heavy at the point, it shows obstinacy.

If short, comparatively, it indicates indecision, a weak will, easily ruled by others; the subject may be reasonable, if second phalange is long, but will be a castle builder, rarely putting into execution the ideas, yet a good counselor to others, though he will not profit by it himself. Such an individual will make magnificent plans, but lack determination, not possessing sufficient will to carry out or put into execution his plans.

If the first phalange is nearly as long as the second, and the thumb compared with the rest of the hand is strong and of good length, it will give a fine character, able to execute excellent plans, ruling with reason, being loved by servants and relatives, an industrious nature, logical, with a love of perfection in work.

The native respects law and order, with reason in argument.

A short, clumsy, thick-set first phalange representing a club, denotes animal instincts, coarse, brutish ideas, a lazy, gross and obstinate person, who cautiously awaits his opportunity for any deed of violence.

The second phalange, between the first and second joint, should be long and strong, not too thick, but showing a slight tendency towards a waist-like form; this indicates more refined thought than a very thick formation;

it gives strong reasoning propensities, good arrangements and plans, thoughtfullness and ability.

The third phalange, called the mount of venus, which occupies a portion of the palm, when long, high and encroaching, the subject will possess a large share of the passionate and sensual side of nature. This with a weak first and second, gives little or no hope of a good character, having neither will nor reason to guide the animal nature.

With the second long and first short, the third will be controlled by reason, but there will be a continual struggle between right and wrong, reason being feeble because will is weak.

The first long and the second short, the will power controls from sheer force, such power being forcible in the gratification of selfish desires; if with a short head line, reason will not aid, therefore lacking the necessary combination; with a long head line the subject will be firm and constant.

A weak and flat third phalange is indicative of poor health, a cold and undemonstrative disposition, lacking affection. If with a poor mount of Jupiter and weak heart line, selfishness is prevalent; and if soft there is a lacking of vital force and energy.

When medium developed, it signifies strong, pure affections; if also elastic when pressed, good health and strong constitution, a system not likely to be drained by excesses.

When the thumb stands off the hand at right angles, the nature will fly to extremes from absolute independence of spirit, the native will detest control, and cannot be advised; consequently is liable to loose money and enter into projects disastrous—to their own detriment.

The thumb well formed and lying in a cramped position towards the fingers, shows entire want of independence; such is indicative of a nervous, timorous, but cautious nature, very reserved. One can never anticipate what such a person is about to do.

When the first joint is supple, allowing the phalange to bend back from the hand, it denotes liberality; but if extreme it shows extravagance, a spendthrift, improvident of time, a very erratic nature, not so cautious or strictly moral as the firm-jointed thumb; but very adaptable to new places and things, strange people or new countries, soon feeling at home.

The stiff-jointed thumb, denotes prudence and good sense. The possessor will be found practical, cautious and secretive, strong willed, determined and a go-ahead disposition with a stubborn determination to succeed; the character will be found stronger than the supple joint which leaps and bounds, whereas this development is content to proceed step by step. Such a person is strong in rule, possessing great self-control, yet in love undemonstrative but staunch, possessing a keen sense of justice.

If the hand is hard, the tendency towards firmness and energy indicated will be increased, and a person with the first phalange developed will be more firm of purpose in execution of plans than the soft hand.

Soft hands use their wills more by fits and starts, and are not to be depended upon.

With the first phalange long, they will work because it is a duty and not because they love it.

Long first phalange, a man governed by the faculty of will.

Long second phalange, a man governed by intellect and the reflective functions.

Long third phalange, a man governed by his feelings and faculties of affection.

THE FINGERS AND JOINTS.

When smooth they are indicative of impulse in thought, a subject guided by intuitions, jumping rapidly at conclusions without weighing or studying out matters carefully, generally acting upon first thought.

Smooth, pointed or conical, belong to dreamers and poets. The possessors of such are lacking in practical understanding.

When smooth and square, modifies matters, making a more scientific individual endowed with power of organization, being fond of literature and art. A lover of order without practicing it.

When smooth and spatulate the productions are as described in the different formations, inventions, mathematicians and astronomers are found.

Both finger joints, when knotted, indicate justice in judgment, order and punctuality, a subject not easily influenced by sentiment, exercising method in action through reflection.

When knotted and conical, aptitude is indicated for science and philosophy.

Knotted, square signifies thoughtfulness, faithfulness, progress, a love of justice, harmony and jurisprudence.

Knotted, spatulate makes the nature ambitious, courageous, practical and active.

Knotted and pointed indicates an observant nature,

loving reality and truth; refined in manners; appreciating the beautiful. Yet there is often a fight between their inspirations and faculties of analysis. Originality in art without success.

Individuals with the first joint only knotted are philosophers and deep thinkers. Where the lower joint is the only knotted one, the nature is limited to material and a lover of order in business affairs and management. If on a spatulate hand, it gives a love of machinery. To musicians knots give rythm and to priests strength of resistance and version.

Pointed hands and smooth joints are purely intuitive, often careless about dress and appearance, for they cannot be troubled with detail.

Long fingers love detail in every branch, the finishing touches with exactness in small matters. The possessor of long fingers has good memory; being fond of argument and can learn by heart freely.

Short fingers are the reverse. They cannot be troubled with detail, therefore take things as granted without examination. Their nature is more impulsive and hasty. In case of them being smooth and transparent a chatterbox is produced.

When short, thick and clumsy, the faculty of selfishness is indicated, attended with cruelty.

When stiff and curved inward, excess of prudence and avarice is signified. This makes the individual overcautious and also denotes a cowardly disposition.

Supple and bent back they tell of a nature charming in company, affable and clever, but curious and inquisitive, fond of gossiping and generally extravagant in money matters.

Crooked or twisted fingers on a bad hand indicate cruelty and an evil nature. A fleshy ball or substance on the inside nail phalange indicates extreme sensitiveness. The subject exercises tact through the dread of causing others pain.

When thick and puffy at base, it is a man of greediness; the individual considers his own comfort before others, naturally over fond of good things, drinking and eating, desiring luxury. On the contrary, when shaped at the base, waist-like, it shows an unselfish disposition and attention to cleanliness and daintiness of food.

When fingers open wide between first and second, it shows independence of thought; likewise if third and fourth open wide, independence of action. Both very wide, originality and self-reliance, and if the fingers naturally curl up towards the palm, when so held, the subject will be conventional.

The fourth finger, if well shaped and long, acts as a compensation or balance to the thumb, indicating power to influence others.

If very long, it gives great power of expression, in both writing and speaking, and the possessor is more or less a philosopher, conversing with ease on any subject. He can interest his associates, commands people by the application of facts, respecting anything brought to his attention on the subject of debate.

NAILS.

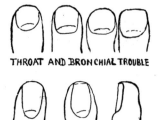

THROAT AND BRONCHIAL TROUBLE

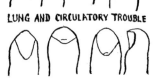

LUNG AND CIRCULATORY TROUBLE

TENDENCY TOWARD PARALYSIS.

When long denote less physical strength than a nail of a short broad type. Very long, if ribbed, show chest and lung troubles. If much curved from the top back towards the fingers, they indicate consumption and tendency to weak lungs. This also will show spinal complaint.

The above mentioned nails, when short, will indicate throat trouble, bronchial affections and asthma.

Long nails, very wide at the top, with a bluish tint, denote bad circulation, ill health and nervous prostrations. Women between the ages of 42 and 47 often have this indication. Long almond nails are not malicious, but sweet tempered.

Long nailed persons are less critical than short, and are more impressionable. Their physical nature is weaker, especially if thin; they show more resignation and calmness in every way.

Short nailed individuals will look facts in the face, whether pleasant or unpleasant. They are critical, especially in matters relating to self; having keen perceptions, an artistic nature; inclined to logic and reason; are fond of argument; will hold out to the last, and not yield a point until compelled. Always on the alert for humor, and the ridiculous; quick and sharp in temper.

When broader than long, it shows a fighting temper, a pugnacious disposition, and a tendency to worry and meddle with other people's affairs. If square at the bottom, passionate anger.

Small and short nails give tendency to heart disease, especially if thin and without moons.

When small nails are flat, white and brittle, having an inclination to turn up on the outer edges; these are fore-runners of paralysis.

Short, flat and sunken at the base, as if it were in the flesh, show nervous disease.

Nails that are both short and wide indicate false-hood and cunningness; a weak moral nature.

Large moons show good circulation.

Bitten nails indicate a worrying disposition, irritable temper; the best that can be said of this, is that it is a filthy habit.

Black spots upon the nails, show grief and melancho-ly while they last.

White spots show the nervous system wants rest and attention.

The following is not always to be relied upon.

White marks on the thumb nail are said to show some strong mutual attachment; a black spot, some crime through passion. White spots on first finger nail, a gain. Black spot, a loss.

Middle or second finger nail. A white spot there-

on indicates a journey; black mark, some downfall loom-
ing.

White spot on the third finger nail, honor and
money; black mark, infamy in store.

THE LOCATION AND NAMES OF THE MOUNTS AND FINGERS AS REPRESENTED BY THE PLANETORY INFLUENCES.

All the mounts being equal in size show harmonious character.

The mounts are indicated by the slight swellings, sometimes quite prominent inside the palm, below the fingers.

Mount Venus is located at the root of the thumb, spoken of elsewhere as the third phalange.

The mount of Mars, number one, is situated over Venu- (see Diagram No. 23), the life line generally separating it from Mount Jupiter, which is at the root of the Jupiter finger, the first or index finger.

Mount Saturn is located at the root of the finger of Saturn, which is the second.

Mount Apollo is situated at the root of the ring finger, which is the third on the hand.

Mount Mercury is situated at the root of the finger of Mercury, which is the fourth.

The Mount of Mars, No. 2, may be found on the percussion as indicated in (Diagram, No. 23).

The Mount of the Moon will be found below that of Mars.

According to the developments of the mounts and fingers, whether small, large or well developed, the characteristics may be delineated.

Diagram No. 15.

JUPITER.

The mount of Jupiter well developed, indicates reverence, ceremony and pomp, sense of honor, religion, ambition, love of rule, enthusiasm in undertakings and aspirations for justice

When found on a square hand with a good mount, it shows a great mind, love of regularity and established authority.

The undevelopment or absence shows idleness, ignorance, vulgarity, a selfish and irreligious nature, lacking in dignity.

If abnormal or excessive, gives pride, dominant in spirit, and extravagant, love of display; and with pointed fingers, superstition.

Jupiter well developed will always be pageant to great mindedness.

The Finger of Jupiter.

The finger should be of fair length, straight, in proportion with other fingers, which is indicative of thought and economy.

When abnormally long the subject will have unusual desire to rule with tyranny over others, and an excessive amount of pride.

When as long as the second or middle finger, it then signifies a keen sense of luxury, even to sensualism, love of pleasure, and a subject ashamed of poor relatives.

When short, the significations are love of activity with sudden decisions.

A long and pointed first finger is indicative of comprehension, intuition, love of reading, and if the hand is good their religious faculties will be fully developed; if pointed, with others square and a good line of Sun, the person will be of an artistic nature, and serious.

A square tip gives exactitude of thought and habit (symmetry).

When found spatulate, it indicates much activity, locomotion, a love of manual exercise and of animals, war, commerce and agriculture.

The first phalange long, denotes perception and religion.

The second long, indicates learning, events, and ambition.

The third, when long, betrays pride, wisdom, and love of rule.

My experience is, if the finger of Jupiter be as long as the second, life is ruled by ambition.

If all are short, the fingers may be judged as lacking thought.

SATURN.

The mount of Saturn well developed, indicates prudence, sober judgment, good sense, calmness, naturally cautious with a tendency to occult science.

The absence or when small and flat, denotes insignificance in life, one who is continually suppressed by a sense of misfortune.

Excessively developed or abnormal the indications are a sad, remorseful nature, having a horror or fear of death, yet a morbid curiosity which often leads to suicide. The subject loves to be alone, often a religious fanatic.

The Saturnian Finger.

This is the second or middle finger. When highly developed or excessive, it indicates remorse, sadness, morbid imaginations and melancholy, especially if long and flat, and when twisted, murderous inclinations are existing.

This finger when pointed, modifies the sad and morbid influence, produces frivolity and callousness, with a tendency to counterbalance the moroseness, especially if the hand is the owner of a small thumb.

The square Saturnian finger is indicative of prudence, a great character; and when long and square the disposition is grave and stern.

When found spatulate, there will be great activity, excessive imaginations, and morbid tendency reflecting upon the spiritual world. It also denotes love for horses, when long.

The first phalange long, gives dignity during adverse circumstances and great temptation to commit suicide.

The second phalange, if long, indicates a love of agriculture, and mechanical occupations; and if knotted a love of science in all its details.

The third phalange long, signifies practical treatment, with avarice.

When the end or tip inclines toward the first finger, it gives fatalism modified by self confidence; if it inclines toward the third or middle finger, fatalism is dominated by art.

THE SUN.

The mount of Apollo or Sun, gives instinct, love of art, producing a subject of genius possessing amiability, enthusiasm, with appreciation of the beautiful, a love for splendor, formal religious ceremonies, poetry, painting, literature and unity, possessing glory, celebrity and brilliancy of fortune; such subjects love to shine before the world, exercising grace of mind and thought.

When undeveloped, insignificance, a dull unenlightened life and intellectual lassitude.

When abnormal, an extravagant, boasting, lying, envious nature, with an unreasonable temper.

The Finger of Apollo or Sun.

(The Ring Finger.)

This finger denotes riches, art and fame. When longer than the first, the significations are artistic, a boasting individual, with much ambition to become notorious, celebrated and wealthy. If, however, it is as long as the second, a gambler is produced, a person foolhardy and rash, especially when the mount of Mercury is developed. Of course, if the other part of the hand is good and strong, it indicates much enterprise and adventure, especially if the finger tips are spatulate.

When pointed, intuition in art matters, are denoted, artistic feelings, and if the others are not pointed that person may be considered frivolous and a boaster.

This finger, when square; much research and reason in art is indicated, but with bad lines an extreme desire for riches will prevail. On the contrary when a good hand, it tells of truth and reason in art, life being somewhat devoted for the money there is in it.

When spatulate; gives love of form, a charming figure well formed appeals to their eyes; it also gives dramatical and sensational talents. Artists possessing this formation will be painters of animals and historical subjects.

The first phalange long, indicates love of display, art and colors.

The second phalange long, indicates industry and love of work, respecting art.

The third phalange comparatively longer than the

others, betrays love of form and conventionality, vanity
and great desire for wealth.

When this finger is found abnormal or excessively developed, the subject may be termed a gambler, who looks
upon life as a lottery.

MERCURY.

This mount when well developed, gives commercial aptitude, fondness for exact science, cheerfulness, intelligence, love of change, travel, and excitement. It also is the indicator of wit, giving promptness in thought and expression, and desire for the association of the young; with Venus well developed, men often marry young wives. If on a good hand, the qualities indicated are to the individual's benefit, but if on a bad hand, to his detriment.

This mount when deficient, gives a lack of intelligence and a negative life.

When excessive, it denotes theft, deceit, treachery, a person who searches for false and dishonest occultism.

Finger of Mercury.

This finger may be termed the finger of expression and it should be straight and long, which would enable the individual to twist his associates, as the saying goes "Round his little finger." It should rise above the first joint of the companion finger. When crooked, it gives a tendency to fanaticism.

When pointed; gives tact, eloquence, diplomacy; excessively so, produces trickery.

When square; logic and common sense in science, speech, abundance, simple and to the point; good teachers and business men have this formation.

When spatulate; a love of scientific problems, machinery, and mechanical skill.

The first phalange long, indicates eloquence, a great talker combined with skill.

The second when long, gives a love of occultism of human nature, strong argumentive powers with industry.

The third phalange shows cunningness, lying, desire for adventure, and if as long as the third finger, a deceiver and cheat.

Diagram No. 19.

MARS.

There are two Mounts of Mars; No. 1, inside life iine and No. 2, near Mercury (see Diagram, No. 23).

No. 1, when well developed, endows the native with active courage and bravery. A brave, gallant, aggressive individual, possessing hardihood of nature being very self-possessed in time of danger or an emergency.

When excessive; violence and insolence are denoted. A quarrelsome, fighting disposition. loving danger for danger's sake.

When small; cowardice, timidity, a nature lacking presence of mind.

People who occupy governmental positions, soldiers, miners and dealers in iron, steel and sharp instruments, generally have the Mount of Mars large.

No. 2; Mount of Mars, near Mercury, denotes self-control, resignation in misfortune, strength of resistance against injustice.

The subjects of Mars, when found among servants, are liable to break the crockery and damage the drawing room. They are not afraid to run great risks and they generally look after their stomachs.

Diagram No. 20.

THE MOON.

Luna developed, indicates refinement and imagination. A nature delighting in lovely scenery; endowed with taste for poetry. A lover of romantic life, tropical scenery, etc. A fondness for mystery and emotional literature, given to dreams, often lazy, thus scattering their abilities.

When excessive; it produces diseased imagination; a superstitious, irritable, sad and discontented nature, which produces headaches.

When small and flat, they may be summed up as severe in judgment of others, lacking imagination, sympathy and ideas.

The subjects of the Moon, are often influenced by their sexual propensities and success is indicated in dealings with public commodities.

Diagram No. 21.

VENUS.

The mount of Venus attributes attraction for the opposite sex, love and worship, beauty, grace, charity and affection.

If well developed, indicates strong and robust health with ability to comfort the unhappy, giving warmth and energy, love of beauty and grace of manner, and desire to please.

The absence of this mount or when undeveloped betrays ill health, coldness, lack of tenderness and love.

Abnormally large; inconstancy, coquettry, idleness and a violent passion for the opposite sex. Situated on a hard hand, it gives wit and grace of manner.

The subjects influenced by the planet Venus are lovers of pleasures and well adapted to social life. They love gaiety, song and melody, and are apt to jump rapidly at conclusion. They desire to give pleasure, rather than seek approbation. Their nature being humane, gentle and docile.

COMBINATIONS.

Frequently the mounts are found out of their proper places, leaning towards each other, which makes a combination, with one another, as it were combining the qualities together.

The mount of Jupiter and Saturn predominant, shows good luck through life.

Jupiter and Mercury, gives a love of science.

Jupiter and Venus strong; unselfishness in their devotion to the opposite sex, pleasant, sociable, sincerity in affections, honest, pure love.

Jupiter and the Moon, predominant; a just and passive disposition, sober and honest.

Saturn and Sun, largest (with good lines); shows veneration with a good heart.

Saturn and Mercury (with good lines); a thirst for knowledge, science and medicine; in a bad hand, a cheat and nasty disposition.

Saturn and Mars, predominant; gives aggressiveness, a fighting spirit, a don't care, unforgiving nature.

Sun and Mercury, gives a firm loving nature.

Sun and Venus; amiability, great wish to please and obliging, genial and expressive devotion.

Sun and Moon an imaginative, calm, poetic and musical nature, with talents limited to imaginative work.

Sun and Mars; perseverance in the direction of art

and a love of scientific truth. Aggression and a warlike temper.

Mercury and Venus, ruling (with good lines); fine flow of language tinged with ideality, an affectionate disposition.

Mercury and Moon (in a good hand); a schemer, but usually a tricky person, fond of change and new surroundings, not particularly honest.

Mercury and Mars most prominent, gives quickness of thought.

Venus and Moon (in a woman's hand); liability to elopement, liking romantic love affairs.

Moon and Mars; love of navigation.

Venus and Mars; sensuality and jealousy.

Diagram, No. 22.

PART II.

CHEIROMANCY.

Diagram No. 23.

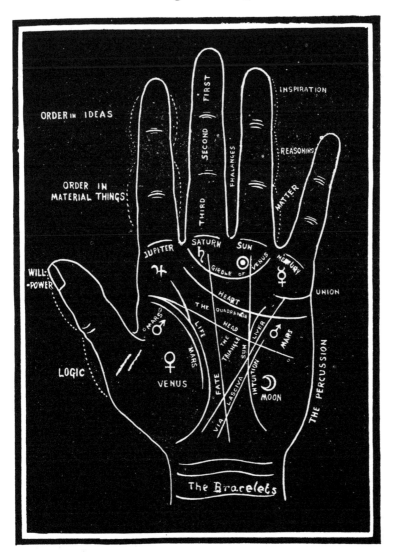

The Map of the Hand.
THE LINES.

THE LINES.

" What evil is in my hands?"—*Sam. xxvi:16.*

The lines may appear, fade and disappear, change their color and grow shorter and longer. They should be clear and well marked, neither broad nor pale, and free from encumbrances.

A single evil mark must not be accepted as conclusive, for any serious evil will always be supported by other lines if carefully examined.

When the lines are pale, they signify that the subject is of a feminine nature, lacking robust health, and determination; mentally and physically weak.

When the lines are red, good circulation and vivid mentally, a sanguine, hopeful disposition is indicated.

Yellow lines are often temporary and signify biliousness, poor circulation, and a melancholy nature. The possessor of such are generally reserved and proud.

Black or dark lines betray a grave, melancholy temperment, such a native will be revengeful, haughty, distant and of an unforgiving nature. Long fingers strengthen these qualities.

The sister lines are those running parallel to the main lines; they give increased power, support, defense; strengthening and bridging over a break, preventing danger that may be indicated.

Lines when forked at the end, signify increased power, with indications of a dual nature, this applies to all lines except the life line.

The tasseled lines are signs of weakness; such depreciate the part or qualities indicated.

Branch lines rising are good indications, giving strength and abundance of qualities pertaining to the line.

When rising from the head line; intelligence, talent and cleverness.

When from the heart line, worthy affections.

Rising from the line of Saturn, good luck.

The descending lines are detrimental; just the reverse to those ascending.

The ascending lines from the commencement of the heart are of great importance with regards to success in marriage; for such denote increased warmth of affections, vigor and power in that direction.

The lines if found chained in their formation, signify obstacles, trouble and weakness, for instance in heart, changeableness in affections.

The head lacks of fixity of ideas and weak intellect.

Broken lines are indicative of failures, and when wavy the power of that line is reduced.

Capillary lines in most cases denote weakness, obstacles and ill success; in the same way as the chained.

When the hand is found covered with a number of small lines like network, it is a sure sign of a mental, nervous temperament, mental worry and a troubled nature.

LIFE LINE.

The length of the individual's existence may be determined by this line; also sickness, and constitutional strength.

It should be long, completely encircling a good mount of Venus (the ball of the thumb); free from irregularities, breaks and cross-lines. Not too fine and not too broad; but deep and narrow. Such predicts good health, long life and a strong constitution.

The variance of this line in thickness, indicates a fickle disposition, and capriciousness.

When the line is pale and broad is signifies poor instincts, ill health and an envious nature.

When red, deep and broad, the temper is repulsive and the will violent. There is an ascendency of the brute kind.

When pale and shallow, of a chain like appearance (Diagram 27, No. 9), it denotes a delicacy of constitution; especially on a soft hand. The part where the line recovers its evenness, health is regained.

Uneven and chained, low down the hand, signifies bad health during the native's latter days. If at the commencement, bad health in early life.

The shorter the line, the shorter the life, and death may be predicted according to the termination of the lines in both hands.

Illness may readily be announced, when a broken line is found, and if in both hands great danger of death;

especially if the inner branch turns inward towards mount Venus (Diagram 25, No. 12). A broken line with the end joining the fate line, may be said to be an accident averted by good luck.

A break in one hand and not in the other, may only be termed a danger, unless supported by other influences, such as a break in the head and fate line; likewise if in one hand the life line terminates and in the other continues the time of death may not be predicted as an absolute certainty, the one line containing Mars, may preserve life.

The health line should also be taken into consideration as to its sloping position, and in many cases will indicate the disease.

When the line is continually crossed by small short lines or bars, a sickly and weak subject is the result.

When the life line stops short with a few small parallel lines (Diagram 25, No. 11), it is an indication of death.

If the line be broken up in pieces (Diagram 25, No. 15), it is a certain sign of delicacy in health and sickness while it lasts.

When broken inside a square (Diagram 24, No. 17), it denotes preservation and recovery from a serious iliness or accident.

A bar across the end (Diagram 24, No. 18), signifies preservation from illness.

Lines crossing from mount Venus to life line are worries and troubles, caused by others, such as financial affairs with relatives, litigation or illness, through a loved one.

A ray line from Venus just cutting life line, may indicate marriage, the date as shown on life line.

Numerous short cross lines on the life line show illness and headaches.

When the extremity of the line appears wavy and tasselled (Diagram 24, No. 16), it signifies loss of substance and money late in life; likewise if found tasselled and extending to the mount of Luna, eventual insanity may appear or danger of folly resulting from those troubles. The extending line to mount Luna is shown by (Diagram 24, No. 14).

A sister line (Diagram 25, No. 8), may always be looked upon as an indication of strength, counteracting the evil effects or irregularities which may be found on a main line.

The origination of lines from mount Jupiter connected with the life, shows boundless ambition from youth.

The lines should be free from forks and tassels, irregularities and obstacles through their course, with the exception of a well formed branch on mount Jupiter, which will indicate on a good hand justice of heart, fidelity, ambition, etc., (Diagram 25). The two little branches from commencement are indicative of vanity and indecision.

A single distinct fork at the end of the life line gives a tendency to overwork during old age.

A fork or branch running to the line of Head (Diagram 25, No. 21), equals faithfulness, but when it branches from the centre of the line; especially if the head line be weak or the branch tasselled (Diagram 27, No. 11); shows diminished force, a relaxation of efforts.

Many ray lines branching across the hand from mount Venus are indicative of worries and troubles.

A line from the mount of Venus (Diagram 24, No. 19), signifies marriage at the turn indicated on the life line.

Branches or ray lines crossing to line of Fortune to a star in the triangle show loss of money.

When crossing over to line of Head, a consequent loss of reason or mental weakness.

If extending to the Sun line and cutting it (Diagram 24, No. 6), it indicates worry, loss of money, ruin or misfortune of one's parents; and if it commences from a star on mount Venus, misfortune is caused through death of parent.

If an island appear on the line (Diagram 24, No. 20), the results are, or have been serious, and if there be a fork at the end where No. 20 line cuts the life line it indicates an unhappy marriage.

The life, head and heart lines when much joined together at commencement signify a tendency to deception. Such a native through intellectual defects and for want of perception rushes headlong into danger, and the subject will stick at nothing to gain his ends as regards affections. It is a sign of misfortune.

When the life line divides or shoots out a branch to the commencement of mount Luna on a good firm hand, it indicates prolonged desires with the realization of long voyages, but when found on a soft and flabby hand with sloping head line, the individual will be too lazy to gratify his cravings in this direction, therefore directing his desires to vice and intemperance.

A line branching from the life line to mount Jupiter (Diagram 24, No. 9), indicates ambition, and if found on both hands, a rise in position or gratified ambition, if not otherwise crossed off, the date may be taken from life line. A small cross right at the end of the line is exceedingly good. The branch line when forked on a good mount of Jupiter, gives justice of heart and fidelity; the contrary, a bad hand, vanity and indecision.

When forked, starting from the side of hand inconstancy; and if commencing from head line forked, faithfulness.

Small line drooping from life line signifies weakness, loss of vitality, poverty or loss of character.

Branch lines that rise from life line (Diagram 25, No. 21), are indicative of dignity, gain, success and increased power.

A branch line running from a black spot, signifies that a disease has left a nervous complaint, for black spots always indicate disease, and when very deep, death may often be predicted.

A branch line from life rising to mount of Saturn, running parallel with the fate line is indicative of much wealth and wordly goods, resulting from the subject's own determination, efforts and energy.

A ray line crossing over to Saturn show accidents from animals; especially if it branches at the end.

A line ascending to Apollo from life indicates celebrity, distinction, success in art, according to class of hand. Indistinct ray lines to this mount are not good.

When branching to mount Mercury it gives success in business, inventions, science, etc., generally the result of personal merits, determined by the formation of hand, spatulate, conic or otherwise.

Good lines running parallel by the side of life are favorable.

Such a line when entangling itself with the life line indicates great success, vigor and riches.

Again oblique lines cutting life line are obstacles and troubles caused by opponents, interferences with the native's life.

Lines cutting life line only may be termed interferences of relatives in domestic life.

Many small cross lines, a delicate constitution, prolonged illness. One heavy, short line, bronchial troubles; generally asthmatic.

A line crossing from life and running to the fate line shows opposition with business and worldly intercourse, the date of which must be taken from the fate line, where the line cuts it.

A ray or cross line from life to the head signifies brain difficulties, mental disorders or people who will dominate our thoughts and interfere with our ideas of opinions.

When crossing over and cutting heart line, obstacles and interferences with private matters pertaining to our affections or illness caused through affairs of the heart, the date is given on the life line.

When extending to and cutting the sun line, it indicates interferences of others who will spoil our position in life, causing mischief or scandal; if an island appears at the end, public scandal will be the result.

A line cutting life and head line with a star between, signifies loss of reason; the date should be observed.

An island on life line denotes an illness while it lasts or loss of vitality, generally shown on the hand, caused by excesses elsewhere.

An island clearly formed at commencement of life line signifies a mysterious birth, a native born under peculiar circumstances.

A square is a mark of preservation, while stars and crosses denote trouble.

An oblique line from head line, crossing over to the marriage line, decides a divorce or separation in whose hand it appears, and if this cross line has an island on or near by it, that individual who has caused the separation experienced similar trouble with a person previous to their attachments.

A branch or ray line rising from Mars, low down, cutting the life line, shows illness or trouble, as well as danger brought about through excessive passions, and if starting with many branches, many repeated prosecutions.

This line on a woman's hand is indicative of some unfavorable attachments during her younger days, the result of which created a source of troubles.

This same line sending out branches to the life line shows continual prosecution at different intervals. The man that influenced her would have a firey, passionate, animal nature.

If the ray line should travel by the side of it, it shows on a female's hand that the man who enters into her affections has the gentler nature, and that she will have the stronger influence in their relationship.

If the line, when travelling with the life line, retreats farther at the end away from the life line into the mount of Venus, it indicates that the individual whom the woman is connected with will gradually lose sympathy with her and eventually drift away.

When this influence line ends suddenly and then reappears, it shows that the influence over her life will terminate in disgrace.

When it fades away gradually and then reappears, it shows that the person influencing her life will cease his influence at that point, but it will be renewed again.

When the line of influence fades altogether, total separation, or death, will result.

When it joins a cross line and runs over the hand with it, it foretells that through another, the affections of the person influencing the life will change to hate, and this will cause injury at the point it touches the life, fate, head or heart line.

The further the ray line is from the life line, the further removed from the native's life will those influences be.

Numerous such influence lines near the life line indicate a nature dependent upon affection; such people are called sensual.

A cross line from the passive mount of Mars extending to the life line generally indicates a wound.

A circle on the life line often indicates blindness or serious eye trouble.

A line of life, when lying close to the thumb, indicates sterility, especially if the line of head and health are joined together by a star.

A line of life dividing towards the end, near the wrist, with a wide space between the lines, indicates the native will end his days in a different country from that of his birth, or there will be some great change from the place of birth to the place of death.

THE HEAD LINE.

There are two hemispheres on the hand, mind and matter, which are divided by this line.

The line of the head, cerebral or mentality, when in unison with the other characteristics, gives more constancy, enthusiasm and originality.

When pale and broad, feebleness of intellect, indecision, but with a good thumb and mount of Mercury he should be cautioned against overwork.

If chained, a want of fixity of ideas, changeableness.

If so very short, terminating, as it were, under the mount of Saturn, early and sudden death.

Twisted and unevenly marked and of a bad color, feebleness of spirit, an avaricious nature.

When full of little islands and hair lines, it signifies danger of a diseased mind and pain to the head.

If the line turns to any particular part or mount of the hand, it partakes of that quality. To mount Jupiter, vanity, pride, ambition for power, and with a star on the mount success is realized. To mount Saturn, a leaning towards music, depth of thought and religion. The Sun, great desire for notoriety. Mercury, gain in business affairs, commerce, science. If ending between the third and fourth finger, art and science combined. To mount Luna, a love of occult, mysterism and imagination.

This line when running from mount Jupiter, slightly separated from the life line and extending well across the

Diagram No. 24.

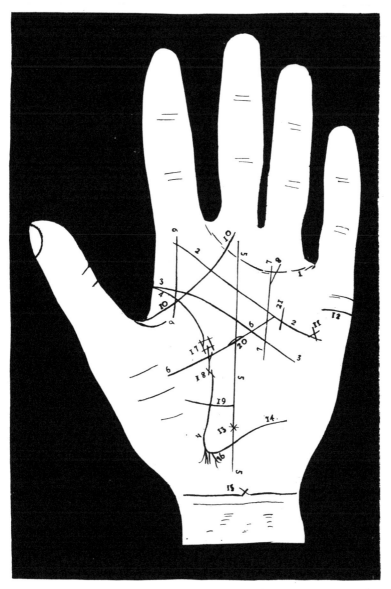

Line Map of the Hand.

hand, indicates intelligence, self reliance and personal as-surance, a good amount of dash and a go-ahead spirit. And if it slightly connects with the head line, just touching it, the native will take great pride in managing and ruling others, having great determination, combined with reason, yet ruling with caution and diplomacy.

A moderate space between the two lines at com-mencement (Diagram 28) gives more aggression and free-dom to carry out undertakings and enterprises, signifying promptness of action and readiness of thought.

When very much separated, the individual will jump at decision, running headlong into danger, lacking cau-tion, being hasty, impetuous and foolhardy. If an excessive mount of Jupiter and Mars is added, it gives abnormal self-confidence and recklessness.

When the head line rises from the life line (Diagram 25), being closely connected with it for some distance, such a person lacks self-confidence and the slightest personal re-mark will wound him. He will be extremely sensitive about infringements upon his rights, and too cautious. Yet his life will be guided by reason and intelligence, pos-sessing good abilities. Such people tie themselves down too tightly. There is also a lack of power to exhibit their talents to others just as the time needed. Snubbing will have a bad effect upon such individuals, for they require the contrary - encouragement.

When much connected in the left, self-distrustfulness is indicated. If the right show tendency to separate, the above defect has been conquered by resolution.

A short line with excessive mount of Venus and Moon with a low mount of Jupiter gives laziness.

When pale and broad with low mount of Sun, a dull intellect.

When made up of little islands with fluted nails, curved at top, consumption.

A poor line with the heart line absent and a wavy liver line, weak heart.

When very weak and narrow, with a poor liver line, irregular, chronic indigestion.

Head line commencing from heart line with a liver line originating from life, a tendency to fainting fits.

A good line with a broad quadrangle, a conical finger of Jupiter, others square is a sign of thoughtfulness.

A line long and straight with a good heart line and a well developed finger of Jupiter gives economy with avariciousness.

When the head line is found rising from the mount of Mars within the life line, the indications are a fretful, worrying, irritable temper, with inconsistency in thought and actions: the possessors of such will always be in conflict with their associates or relatives, manifesting a disagreeable trait of character.

When clear, even and straight, good reasoning powers are denoted with practical common sense, a nature more successful with material rather than the imaginative, and if long fingers, a love of detail.

When the first half is straight and the remainder is sloping, it signifies that the balance between practical and imaginative work is good. The owner of such a line would commence imaginative work on a practical basis, going about his business in a common sense way.

The whole line continuing to slope shows an imaginative turn of mind as may be indicated by the formation and other signs of the hand; music, painting, literature or inventions.

A very sloping line gives romance and sentiment, sometimes illusions and folly. If a fork branches on the regions of Luna, it denotes imaginative literary talents, an impractical nature. When exceptionally long, the native may deceive himself, he will also have the ability to deceive others.

If the head line commences from the life line under Saturn, it indicates that the development of the brain and the subject's education has been acquired late in life.

An exceptionally good head line, supported by a good mount of Mars, will often be found to dominate over other evil signs in the hand.

When the line is extremely long, running right over the hand, it shows unusual development of the mental facilities, and that person will be aware of his superior intellect; and selfishly inclined with the use of it.

The same line when turning up at the end towards Mars indicates that the native will gain great business success. He will take care of his money and substance, having a keen sense of its value.

A short line to about the centre of the hand gives a one-sided individual who cannot comprehend two sides of a proposition, lacking intelligence and imagination.

When the head line is placed high on the hand, making a

larger hemisphere of matter, the native's desires are then more brutal or animal; when the reverse, the mind predominates.

When the head line rises high upon the hand, taking possession of the heart line or going beyond it altogether, it shows criminal inclinations; such a hand is the attitude of crime, for the subject will stop at nothing to accomplish his purposes when tempted, for his propensities lie waiting for a convenient time to be gratified.

If the connection is under Saturn, say about when 27 years of age; between Saturn and Sun, about 37 years of his life; adding another 10 years if found under the mount of Apollo.

Lines running from the head line towards the heart without touching it, and those from the heart towards the head, show influences of other people over us. Their crossing each other or stopping short, show how far such influences were favorable or detrimental to our happiness.

The lines from the head upwards are those of friendship, while those from the heart may come from love of the opposite sex.

Numerous hair lines branching up to the heart line show fascinated affections rather than love.

When running through a square it preserves the native from violence in love intrigues, through presence of mind.

When the head line is broken in both hands, fatal accidents may be predicted, or violence to the head. If only broken in one hand, the trouble is not so serious.

When it shoots a branch out to the mount of Jupiter, it is an indication of much prosperity and intellectual dominance. A cross line to Saturn, as (Diagram 24, No. 10), is a bad sign, if in a woman's hand, danger of maternity.

When the head line sinks to an abnormal degree on mount of the Moon on the Elementary or Square hand spatulate or philosophic, the first severe shock that is experienced, or when adverse circumstances set in, insanity will result.

The same condition with Saturn excessively developed, melancholy and remorse are liable to appear, until the brain is overbalanced.

Temporary insanity is signified by a narrow island in the middle of a sloping head line, especially with a weakly developed thumb.

When joined to life line and rising towards heart line under Saturn, it gives fatal or blind passion. The line broken just before reaching heart line under mount Apollo, rupture due to foolishness, if under Saturn through fatality.

Broken with a line from heart line to line of Fate, widowhood.

Long and wavy line of head and life; second phalange of finger longer than others, bad teeth.

A branch from head line rising to Jupiter, ambition; Saturn, religious fanaticism; the sun, riches.

A circle on the head line, especially with a cross high up on life line, blindness.

An island on the line with life line, turning red as it approaches it, brain fever.

A line connecting a star on Venus, with a spot on the head line denotes a very serious effect upon the subject through severe disappointment in love.

Capillary lines on the head line, suc has (Diagram 27, No. 13), indicate a good disposition and well balanced mind.

If thin in the centre for a short distance, the result is nervous disease of some kind or neuralgia.

A double or sister head line signifies wealth by inheritance; a double trait of character, both gentle and sensitive, also, cold and harsh. The native will have unusual power of expression and intellectual capacity, with exceptional ability for dealing with human nature.

Diagram No. 25.

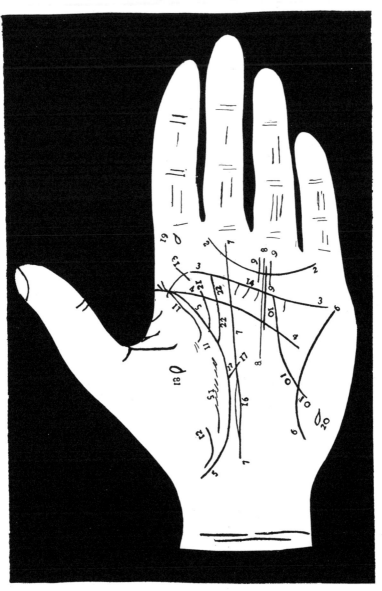

LINE MAP OF THE HAND.

THE HEART LINE.

This line should be well traced, of a good color, deep and clear. Such gives a noble heart, with strong affections.

It is preferable that the heart line should rise from the centre of mount Jupiter, which would show a devotion that is both tender, strong, yet intense.

This particular commencement of the line conduces to an equable disposition, indicative of the highest type of idealistic love, an ambitious character, capable of adoring and choosing the hobby of his heart's desire from among the noble, great and good, whom they wish to make famous.

This line when rising higher up, nearing the finger of Jupiter, is indicative of an excess of the above, such an individual's ambition is in danger of being entirely wrecked by the ideal beauty he may have pictured in his mind as a goddess or even superhuman, through, as it were, blind enthusiasm. He will so devoutly adore his anticipated love that he will forget she is but human, and in case of a disappointment or downfall (for none are perfect), the shock will be so great that he may never recover; therefore, such a person may be said to be totally blind to his intended faults.

A line commencing with a fork on Jupiter, signifies trustworthiness and constancy in love.

Subjects with this line running from Jupiter will have

less love matches than those with the line from Saturn.

This line when found rising from between the finger of Jupiter and Saturn, shows great tenderness; a native possessing a deep love nature of the more passive kind and not so demonstrative, yet sincere; for their passions are quieter and subdued, marriage and home life is their sphere.

When rising from the finger of Saturn it indicates excessive passions in conjugal attachments, with an amount of selfishness for gratifications, and when high up, almost on the finger, sensuality will be prominent.

Not rising from the root of finger, but underneath mount Saturn, a cold heart is denoted, especially if with a low mount of Venus, and if commencing suddenly, without branches, a short life; if very thin, running across the hand, it indicates cruelty, although a native may possess a poor heart line, if he owns a strong thumb and a long headline, matters will somewhat be recompensed through constancy.

The strength of the affections are according to the development and length of the line.

When traced right across the hand, from side to side, blind devotion may result with a production of jealousy and suffering, and if with a high mount of Moon and a ring of Venus, the native will be a victim of unreasonable jealousy.

A chained formation of this line is not good, and with numerous small branches the subject is an inevitable flirt, a lack of sincerity in the wooer, palpitation of the heart may also appear. The same line, with an excessive mount of

Venus, or that mount covered with many cross lines, constant flirtations or even worse may be predicted.

When broad and chained, rising from Saturn, contempt for the opposite sex is the result.

When of a bright red color it indicates an intense, passionate nature, violent in love.

If weak and poorly traced, with a linked head line, faithlessness.

If pale and broad, an indifferent nature.

A line much broken about has a tendency to make a woman-hater, whereas a single break may show feebleness of heart, the results of which may be traced from some excessive mount; if Saturn, excessive fatality; pride if shown by an over-development of the Sun. Folly and avarice is indicated by the mount of Mercury.

The break in the line should be noticed under which mount it appears.

Breaks refer more to the physical state and often indicative of broken engagements, or disappointments in love.

When a break in the heart line is accompanied by a broken head line, it shows heart disease.

Deep scars in the line with an uneven head line, give a tendency to apoplexy.

Broken engagements and heart disease must be carefully distinguished. When the line is of a whitish color and wide under Saturn, appearing blurred, heart disease is the result.

The position of the line with reference to the height, has much to do with the native's happiness.

The elevated position is by far the happier one, for when set low down, but little happiness during early life is experienced.

When out of its normal position, lying close to the head line, matters of the heart are shown to interfere with affairs of the head.

If on the contrary it lies high, the head line narrowing the space between the two lines, exactly the reverse is true. The mentality will then rule the affections and a cold, uncharitable individual, lacking of physical attractions is found.

When the heart line commences with a fork, one branch on Jupiter, the other between the finger of Jupiter and Saturn, it is a good sign, indicating a satisfied, happy, lovable, tranquil disposition.

The same branching on the mount of Saturn gives an erratic nature, attended with much uncertainty respecting happiness in the conjugal life.

Lines rising up from the head line to the heart, indicate influences of the opposite sex and affairs of the heart.

Lines from the quadrangle to the heart line (Diagram 25, No. 14), give aptitude for science and research which does not bring wealth.

An island in the heart line is indicative of illicit love.

The absence of this line is indicative of a selfish dispotion, coldness, hard-heartedness, hypocracy and treachery, especially if the hand is soft; yet they may be sensual.

If the line has faded away, a terrible disappointment may be described, consequently the native may have become cold and indifferent.

A curved line from heart line, branching to mount of the Moon (Diagram 25, No. 10), denotes murderous tendencies and instincts.

When the line is exceptionally thin and devoid of branches, it tells of a cold heart, an emotionless nature.

The absence of this line also shows a nature devoid of affections, it is an evil sign, and such people should be avoided.

When the heart line is much joined to the head and drooping towards that line, it shows a distant disposition, loving stiffness and formality in manners.

When so joined with a cross in the middle of head line, marked in both hands, sudden death will result.

A well developed line with a good mount of Venus and Moon gives a romantic nature.

A poor line of heart and head, with a cross at end of life line, gives untruth.

The line when joined to the head line under Saturn signifies fatal events; under Mercury with an irregular curve, premature death.

When the heart, head and life lines are very much joined together, it is an evil sign, and such people should be avoided.

If the line curls around the first finger it is a sign of occult powers.

A line running to Saturn and suddenly turning back, signifies misplaced affections.

When cut under Mercury with a branch from a cross, failure in business.

If the line turns down on the line of head with a ray

across it (Diagram 25, Nos. 3 and 13), it is a sign of a wretched marriage, or heart grief.

Short lines branching from heart to fate line, broken in their course, indicate widowhood.

Short lines ascending from fate to heart line tell of love and subsequent marriage. If the line touches the base of the finger of Jupiter it signifies unsuccessful undertakings, unless supported by an exceptionally good line of fortune.

A quantity of little lines cutting across the line diagonally, signify misfortunes of the heart, weakness of the heart and liver.

A double line of heart indicates deepest affections that will cause the subject much sorrow.

Diagram No. 26.

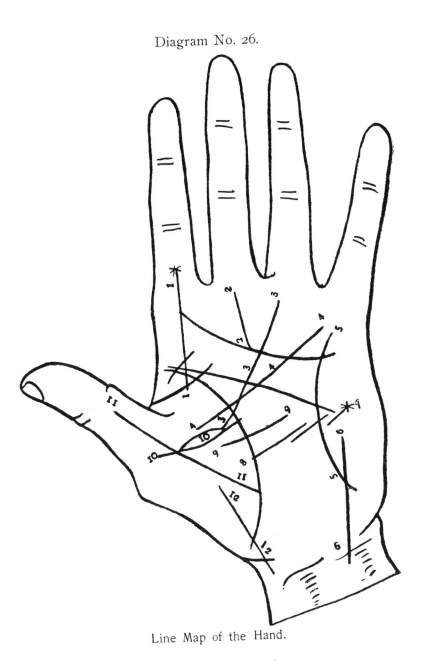

Line Map of the Hand.

FATE LINE, OR SATURNIAN LINE.

The psychic, conic and philosophic hands naturally have this line well developed, therefore, when found upon the elementary, square or spatulate hands the influence is more powerful for good.

It may start from the wrist or from mount Luna, also from life line, centre of palm or head line. It generally partakes of the character of its origin and refers to worldly affairs, success and failures.

It shows people who influence the life, whether for good or evil; joy, money, wisdom or crime, may be measured on this line, also the barriers and obstacles put in the way, and result of the individual's career.

When rising from life line, continuing strong and uncrossed, wealth is indicated by personal energies and merit, but if marked low down near the wrist and tied down by the side of life line, it tells of the early life being sacrificed to the wishes of parents or relatives.

When rising from the wrist and travelling straight up the hand to the mount of Saturn (Diagram 24, No. 5), it gives great success, and if forked, still better; when it runs into the finger of Saturn it gives fatalistic tendencies, every thing goes too far.

The owner of such may be the hero of a great fire, who is disabled for life; or the man who jumps in the water to save his friends at the sacrifice of his own life; or he may be the great leader of men who suddenly turn upon him and take away his life. If this line ends with a star he will run a heroic career, ending with violence or crime.

When rising from Luna, happiness and success will come from or depend much upon others caprice, sometimes public favoritism, actors and notorious characters very often have this line rising from the mount of Luna. Destiny seems to be taken out of the hands of the subjects and remain in the keeping of other people.

When this sign is found in left hand, its absence in the right, the subject has by determination and force, taken his destiny into his own keeping, and freed himself from the interference and control of other people.. But if found joined to the life line in left hand and arising from Luna in right, the subject has willingly handed over his freedom and happiness to another's control.

If a line runs from fate line to Luna, it has a similar meaning viz.: that some person out of fancy or caprice will assist such an individual in his career.

On a woman's hand this line from Luna travelling by the side of fate line denotes wealthy marriage, or influences which will accompany and assist her.

Whenever the line of fate shoots branches out to any particular mount, it indicates that the qualities of that mount dominates the life, and is predictive of success in that direction.

When to the mount of Jupiter gratified ambition, unusual renown, distinction, influence and power will come into the subject's life, people with such an indication are born to rise higher than their fellows. These people may have great energy, but it is still encouraged by success, fortune appears to wait for them to grasp, whereas some others may try and with as much determination to succeed, but obstacles unavoidable prevent success, "such is life." Fate is against them.

If the branch be to Mercury, business gain and scientific triumphs.

When the line terminates by crossing its own mount to that of Jupiter, the success at the end of life is great, giving satisfied ambition.

If the fate line be abruptly stopped by heart line, it shows troubled love, the subject is liable to injure his prospects in life through his affections. Such an individual would be likely to sacrifice a fortune for the sake of marrying the woman he loves.

But when it joins the heart line and together they ascend to mount of Jupiter, the desires and wishes of the happy possessor will be realized.

When the interposition is the head line, it indicates mistaken decisions, wrong judgment; these persons stand in their own light.

Line of fate rising in the plain of Mars or at head line, it shows that the early years of maturity will be full of struggles, the efforts attended with failure, but such is a sign of hope and energy, as the later part of life will be crowned with success. Nevertheless to insure this the line must continue its course unbroken.

When rising from heart line it denotes a successful period after the fiftieth year.

When the fate line throws one branch to mount of Venus, and another to mount Luna, imagination pulls one cord, passion and love pull another, consequently the subject is like a pendulum, and very rarely accomplishes success in life.

If the line be broken, misfortune rules at that period, or while the space lasts.

A line much broken and uneven will show the life of a subject full of ups and downs, joy and sadness.

When chained and torturous, unhappiness brought about by evil deeds.

Upward branches from the fate line show improvement in position and wealth.

If branches tend downward the reverse, pecuniary trouble.

When the fate line is broken with one end commencing before the other finishes, or rather one end wrapping over the other, it indicates a change of residence or business, and such change will prove beneficial. The student must not suppose all breaks in the fate line are evil.

A double or strong sister line is excellent for success, often denoting two distinct careers, a strong influence of another person may be the result and is very important if it branches to other mounts.

A square on the line is a protection from business or financial loss and trouble.

A square touching the line on plain of Mars, foretells danger from accident in relation to home life; if on the side near mount of Luna, it indicates danger of accident while travelling.

A cross is a sign of trouble, and the same rule should be observed with reference to being placed at either side of the line.

An island in the line of fate (Diagram 25, No. 7), shows misfortune and disgrace, sometimes caused by marriage, influence or otherwise. I have known people very successful when the hand contained no line of fate, but they were people who apparently had not very acute sense of feeling, either in happiness or sorrow.

When fate line takes its rise below the bracelet, it indicates great sorrow and tribulation.

Rising from bracelet and terminating at a short head line it is often predictive of business failure.

Broken and cut by numerous lines, continued ill-luck and mischance.

LINE OF SUN OR LINE OF BRILLIANCY.

Indicates glory, prosperity, worldly distinction, artistic or literary talents, and success.

This line may take its origin from mount Luna, the life, fate or heart lines, or from the plain of Mars.

When well formed, long and free from crosses in both hands, gives success and riches. It increases the power of a good line of fate, giving fame and reputation; the source of distinction gained is seen by the termination of the line and other lines of the hand. Otherwise it relates to artistic work, appreciation of art.

If it ends upon its own regions or mount (Diagram No.28), it may give financial success, or fortune from politics, art or law. If terminating on Mercury, the region of utility, the fame is by discoveries, inventions, science or literature.

When rising from the life line, it shows success and fortune gained by inheritance or merit, the lower the line goes the more sure will be the celebrity; with the rest of the hand artistic, it denotes a life worship of the beautiful: with other lines good, it promises success in artistic pursuits.

When rising from the fate line, it increases the success promised by that line, giving more distinction to the person from whatever date marked, or from that time on things will improve.

When rising from mount Luna, it gives success and fame unexpectedly. However, this is still dependent upon the assistance of others, or the caprice of some individual who may take a fancy to assist the native, or through the influence of powerful friends. But this is not to be relied upon when the head line is very sloping, for the subject will lean to poetry, literature and things of an imaginative order, sometimes giving a great tendency to diseased imagination.

Rising upon the plain of Mars (Diagram 25, No. 8), indicates success after many difficulties through personal merit or exertion.

Rising from the head line, there is no caprice or assistance from others, the talents alone of the subject being the factor, but not until late in life.

When rising from the heart line, it shows an appreciative character, loving art and beauty, but not being successful in that direction, either by money or fame. However, it will give some distinction or wealth late in life.

If the third finger is long, nearly as long as the finger of Saturn and there is a long line of Sun, the subject will be passionately fond of risks and will gamble with health, happiness and wealth.

The absence of this line is a sign of difficulty in gaining fame or distinction. Often it is a sign of absolute failure. Even if the subject shows talent, ability and determination, his efforts will probably not meet with any great success.

A square on the line of fortune is a sign of preservation against the attacks of enemies, who may try to assail the reputation and character.

A star on the Sun line is an excellent signal for assistance and good will from others. Brilliant and continued success is sure to result.

An island on this line, for as long as it lasts, means loss of position and name, often through scandal. It is a time when the subject recedes instead of proceeding, when he falls in the estimation of friends, instead of rising.

On a hollow hand the line of Sun loses all power.

A single fork or branch on mount Apollo (Diagram 24, No.8) shows success in one direction, but many branches indicate that efforts are exercised in too many different directions for success and that there is a want of perfection in any. It is rarely that much of importance is achieved, except when the hand shows great force and outstanding talent.

Cross lines are obstacles and if they bar the line near the commencement or wrist, there will be a loss of fortune during youth; or later in life, if higher up the hand.

Any lines which run parallel down the mount in both hands are very good and indicate that success and fame may be obtained.

It is very necessary that a good mount of Jupiter accompany a line of Sun, or there will be success only in money, without any of the favourable qualities of that beneficent mount.

When much broken, the subject is too versatile, with the result that he achieves neither fame nor money.

MARRIAGE LINE.

Civil or ecclesiastical marriages do not register on this line, but marriage of the human body.

The marriage line (Diagram 24, No.12) runs from the percussion side of the hand and takes it course across the mount of Mercury, sometimes drooping towards the line of heart, or taking a curve towards the fingers, these having their separate meanings.

When the line is clear and good, reaching well on to the palm proper, making no curve either up or down, it shows that the married partner will live as long, if not longer than the subject whose hand contains such a line.

My experience has shown that this line does not recognise civil ceremony or ecclesiastical law. The influence is registered from the human body. Its effects are often marked years in advance, upon the percussion or on the face of the mount of Mercury.

Obedience to the law of civilisation, or what may be termed honourable marriage, will be found upon the mount of Jupiter in the form of a distinct cross. Also the fate line or life line will send out an upward branch.

When the marriage line is found drooping at the end towards the heart line, this will indicate that the mate will die first. When a deep cut crosses it, the death is from an accident.

An oblique line running from the lesser triangle to the marriage line indicates there will be a divorce. When the line turns upwards the native will not marry at all.

When a sister line is found with the fate line on the side nearest the life line, with a clear and distinct marriage line, this denotes a fortunate and happy marriage with success.

When the marriage line contains islands the subject should be warned not to marry, as this is a sure sign of much unhappiness.

A branch arising from the upper part of mount Luna and joining the fate line below the line of head, riches and plenty are with marriage.

A forked marriage line shows a broken engagement or separation, while a small line forked, branching from fate line, shows marriage. The lines, which relate to marriage should be clear and strong, of a good length, the shorter ones refer to love affairs or marriage contemplated or influences of the opposite sex.

When the influence line inside the line of life (sometimes called the line of Mars), or the sister line to fate, be stronger than the Saturnian line, the person such a subject marries will be of stronger individuality and more powerful.

An early marriage is indicated when the line is placed low down near the heart line. If situated higher up the hand near the finger of Mercury a late in life marriage may be known by the line. If about the centre, judge the marriage will take place between the ages of 22 and 30. Other signs should be looked for on the fate and life lines for substantiation as to dates.

A delicate, fine line running parallel with the marriage

line signifies some permanent affection after marriage.

When the line is broken it denotes a break in married life, insincerity in union.

A marriage of distinction may be predicted when a line branches from the marriage line to the mount or line of Sun, but if it goes down towards and cuts the line of Sun, the native on whose hand it appears may lose his position through marriage.

When marriage line is clear, with hair lines drooping, it denotes trouble brought on by illness and bad health of the person they have married.

When the line drooping has a cross over the curve, it shows that their partner in life will die suddenly.

CHILDREN.

The lines indicating offspring are the delicate upright or vertical lines from end of marriage lines.

The strongest and clearest lines may be counted as males and the weaker ones females or very delicate children. I have found also the following indications very accurate:

When the lines are found strong at the commencement and gradually growing weaker, they indicate the child was strong at birth and in youth, but became weak and sickly afterwards; but if found the reverse, fain and weak at its connection to the marriage line, then growing stronger, the child was delicate in youth, but became robust and healthy as it grew to maturity.

An island at the end of the line generally denotes death of the child, likewise if found at the commencement it will be sickly.

When one line is superior in length and beauty to the others, that child will be more important than the rest and may be interpreted to be a child with fine mentality.

It is wise to take into consideration the mount of Venus also, as a poorly developed mount is not so likely to have children as a fully developed Venus.

THE HEALTH LINE OR HEPATICA.

The straighter the line the better; but its absence is best for a robust, healthy constitution. Its presence when good, helps to overcome the effects produced by a poor life line. It should start from the bracelet, or from the line of life and go on towards the mount of Mercury, but it is very irregular, and may begin or end almost anywhere in the hand.

When found well colored, narrow, straight and long, it indicates kindly feelings, good memory and health. Some writers consider that when this line starts from the life line, being of equal strength, it foretells a trouble, some disease at work undermining the health.

My experience has not proved the entire accuracy of this statement.

However, it is best for the health line to take its course from the bracelets.

When found running through the life line and stopping at the heart line it shows heart trouble, weak action and poor circulation, especially when pale and broad. Red at the lower end denotes heart weakness; at the upper end, if red near head line, will denote headache or pains in the head and face.

This line terminating at the heart line with nails weak and flat is a sure sign of active heart disease.

When small red or blue spots are seen on this line it

shows tendency to fever. If wavy and irregular, denotes constitutional biliousness, liver trouble, a bad temper.

A sister line avarice. A deep cross bar coming illness, and when broken it will show congestion of the lungs or pleurisy.

Weak digestion is shown when this line is made up of little pieces.

A cross on this line near the head line which contains a circle or island, indicates blindness.

A star near health line in the plain of Mars, shows weak sight and probable blindness.

When numerous islands are seen in this line, with long narow nails, inclining to ribs, consumption and weak lungs are denoted.

In judging this line the student must refer to other lines and notice any indications respecting health and illness for confirmation, such as a chained life line, or heart and nails, etc.

An island on the line, fate line broken in small pieces and no Sun line, shows bankruptcy.

Forming a small triangle with head and fate lines, indicates occultism, intuition and if well defined, clairvoyance.

SOLOMON'S RING.

This gives a love of the occult with directive power in that direction.

LINE OF MARS.

Distinguished as a line running inside the life line, parallel with it.

This line supports the vital forces and will preserve health even when the life line is weak. It provides motivation and will power.

A person with this line (see Diagram 23) on a square or broad hand is extremely healthy, active, excitable and often pugnacious.

When the line of Mars is broad, dark and deep, it indicates passion and violence. If it runs close to the life line, the person will have many conflicts and quarrels, as he is easily annoyed and his fighting instincts quickly aroused. A distinct line of Mars also indicates self assurance and self respect.

A branch extending from this line to mount Luna suggests intemperance in many ways though a superabundance of animal nature which craves excitement.

On a long narrow hand, beside a weak life line, the line of Mars strengthens the life line, supporting it past any serious break.

If this line bridges over a break in the life line, the subject comes close to death at some time in his life but manages to survive.

Soldiers with a strong Mars line are well-suited for military activities.

Finally, a strong line of Mars indicates wealth and prosperity, but violent passions will always be dominant and the subject will know little peace or contentment.

RING OF VENUS.

A rather unfavorable sign (see Diagrams 23 and 24). It gives wit, love, talent for literature and art, making a person highly sensitive, changeable, moody, easily offended and touchy over little things, a highly nervous temperament.

When cut by many small lines, with a large mount of Moon and Venus, it shows despondency, a passionate nature, loving pleasure.

With this mark people are capable of rising to the highest pitch of enthusiasm, but one minute in the highest spirits, the next downcast.

If this line crosses the hand and comes into contact with the marriage line, married life is marred through the peculiarities of the subject, and being so hard to live with. A man would desire more virtues in his wife than there are sands on the seashore.

THE MYSTIC CROSS.

A large cross in the quadrangle. It is found in the upper or lower part and sometimes is formed by the line of fate and another crossing it.

This denotes mysticism, superstition and occultism.

With a short line of head, the subject would be more superstitious than with a long one.

LINE OF INTUITION OR THE LUNA LINE.

(Diagram 26, No. 5; also 25, No. 6.)

This line comes and goes, sometimes in a few months. Its presence being more familiar with the conic and psychic formation.

It signifies an impressionable nature, with psychometric receptibility. A highly sensitive mental temperament.

It influences directly the individuals to strange vivid dreams and presentiments, endowing them with the gift of mesmerism, clairvoyance and thought reading.

When strongly marked with a good head line branching down on mount Luna, it indicates a prophet with brilliant mental conceptions.

An island on this line often makes somnambulists.

Cross lines show voyages.

A star signifies on Luna near the line, a fire at sea or danger of shipwreck.

SATURN'S RING.

This line just encircles the base of the finger.

This ring is not a good sign for success. Individuals possessing such are rarely successful for it appears to cut off their fate.

Such persons may have big ideas and schemes, but lack the necessary power to execute for want of continuity of purpose.

THE LESSER SIGNS.

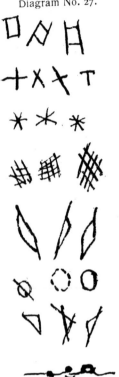

The Square—Preservation, strength, a good sign.

The Cross—Unfavorable, except on Jupiter, which shows happiness in love or marriage.

The Star—Important sign, but generally unfortunate and fatal, except on Jupiter and Apollo, distinction.

The Grill—Confusion, struggles, excesses.

The Island—Hereditary troubles, weakness.

The Circle—On Apollo, glory, elsewhere, entanglement, injury and confusion.

The Triangle—Scientific aptitude, diplomacy, accuracy.

The Spot—Black or blue, nervous illness, disease. If red, injury or wound. If white, some good.

Chained Lines—Irregularities, obstacles.

Broken Line—Illness, interruptions.

Tasseled Line—Feebleness.

Sister Line—Increased power.

Capillary Lines—Weakness, sometimes wounds.

The Lesser Signs.

THE SQUARE.

(Diagram 24, No. 17; also 27, No. 1.)

The line of fate running through a well formed square, will indicate a troublesome time, a financial crisis, but if the line travels directly through a square, all danger is set aside and loss avoided. The conditions arise, but the sign is a symbol of protection, showing that some person or favorable circumstance, prevent the disaster from taking an evil effect.

If out side the line and only touching it, situated under mount of Saturn, it shows protection from accident.

Line of head passing through a square, will indicate weakness or strain from worry, but protecting and helping.

If the line of life be broken in a square, it shows preservation from death or severe illness.

Heart line passing through a square shows troubles through love, but power to bear it.

A square on Venus, indicates protection from trouble brought on by passion, will show the person to be subject to trouble brought on by intrigue and passion, but always managing to escape the consequences.

When found just inside the life line, it is said to mean seclusion from the world, sometimes imprisonment.

When a square is found on any of the mounts, it is said to protect from the excesses of those qualities.

On Jupiter, gives sober sense, and guides the desires represented by that mount.

On Saturn, protects from fatality.

On Sun, the desires and aims protected.

On Mercury, from financial losses.

On Mars, from danger through enemies.

On Luna, from excessive imaginations, or bad effects of other lines.   For instance, drunkenness or travels.

THE CROSS.

On Jupiter; denotes happiness in affection or marriage.

On Saturn; a fatal and adverse influence, tendency to witchcraft and accidents.

On Sun; without Sun line, disappointment in fame and artistic blunders.

On Mercury; disposition to steal.

On Mars; shows dangerous enemies and suicidal tendencies.

On Luna; under line of head, delusions, self-deception and untruthful spirit.

On Venus; some unhappy love affair, a trial, influence of affection, fatal. But if small and lying close to life line, troubles with relatives; on life line, a serious illness.

If found on side of fate between it and life in plain of Mars, shows opposition in the career through relatives.

On the other side near Luna, journeys ending in sorrow.

When found on health line, indicates illness; if on a branch from health line, a change in business affairs.

When on line of head it indicates an accident to the head.

THE STAR.

When on Jupiter, it promises great honour and position, great ambition and gratified love. If at the head, when fate and fame lines are strong, the subject may reach great power and distinction in almost any direction.

On mount of Saturn, it is very evil, indicating some form of terrible death such as assassination, murder, or public execution.

On mount of Sun, it indicates riches and prestige through hard struggle, but little happiness. Riches come too late, the price having been too dearly paid.

The Star on Mercury depends much upon the character of the hand. If the hand is good, it may indicate success in literature. However, if the hand is bad, the Star is a sign of persistent dishonesty. The subject may mix in the best circles of society, but will nevertheless find it difficult to be honest.

On Mars (under Mercury) the Star is usually not a favourable sign. The exception is on a military hand, when it will give distinction in battle, generally through personal bravery.

On Luna, it indicates excessive imagination. The subject will be liable to wild flights of fancy and will be capable of little of a practical nature.

On the first phalange of the thumb, with an excessive mount of Venus, it indicates immorality The subject will have little conscience over gratifying his own desires at the expense of other people's feelings and well-being.

THE GRILL.

(See Diagram 27, No. 24.)

Signification of obstacles, struggles, ill success, taking away the native's good qualities where they may be found.

On the mount of Jupiter, superstition, pride and a dominant spirit is indicated.

On mount of Saturn it foretells misfortune, melancholy and ill-luck.

On mount Apollo it gives absurd vanity, excessive desire for glory and celebrity.

On mount Mercury it betrays cunningness, trickery and dishonesty.

On Mars sudden death, at any rate great danger of such.

On Luna it signifies sadness, a discontented disposition and morbid imaginations.

On Venus it denotes lasciviousness, morbid curiosity, caprice in passion, and if undeveloped, coldness and a want of affections.

On a hand much covered with lines, it indicates an excited state of mind.

A strong first phalange of will power, with a good line of sun and head, counterbalances the effects resulting in excitement.

ISLANDS.

(Diagram 27, No. 5; also Diagram 25, No. 7.)

Islands are local, and generally relate to hereditary troubles, whenever they appear. Heavily marked on heart line, heart disease inherited.

When the island is found on the head line near the center, there is weakness of the intellect inherited.

On life line, it denotes illness at that point.

On fate line (Diagram 25, No. 16), heavy losses in financial matters.

On sun line, loss of good name through scandal.

On health line, sickness and poor indigestion.

When influence lines on Venus run into an island sorrow and disgrace are brought about by the passions.

An island on a line which arises on mount of Venus and crosses life, head and heart lines attacking the marriage line, will indicate trouble in the marital relationship, lawsuits or divorces, caused by a person whose character previously was questionable; at the point crossing the life line, should be counted for time.

When a similar line reaches only to the heart line, disgrace and trouble through the affections.

When the same kind of line reaches the head line (Diagram 26, No. 10), some evil influence will direct the talents and thoughts in a direction, which can only bring disfavor, dishonor and regrets.

Islands on the mounts always impair the good qualities

On Jupiter, weakens the desire for excellence and self esteem.

On Saturn, unfortunate for position and happiness.

On Sun, indicates loss of wealth, and impairs the artistic talent, also is a stumbling block to fame.

On Mercury, too much desire for change in whichever direction the mount inclines.

On Mars, deficient courage, timidity.

On Luna, weakens the sentiment and imagination.

On Venus, easily lead by passion and fancy.

THE CIRCLE AND SPOT.

The circle on mount of Sun is favorable; other mounts unfortunate, showing entanglement and inability to break away.

On Luna it denotes danger from drowning.

When touching any important line, the subject will not be able to clear himself from misfortune; in other words, he will go round and round, not being able to get free.

A spot is generally the sign of temporary illness.

Bright red spot on line of head denotes a shock or injury from accident.

A black or blue spot denotes a nervous illness.

White spots on heart line, conquests in love.

On the head line, discoveries and success.

A bright red spot shows on the health line a fever.

Dot on the end of marriage line indicates widowhood by sudden death.

Spot on mount of Jupiter, damaged reputation.

Spot on the mount of Saturn, evil.

Spot on the mount of Sun, reputation is in danger.

Spot on the mount of Mercury, loss in business.

Spot on the mount of Venus, disease connected with a love affair.

If a spot is found on the life line, it indicates troubles and sickness through a love affair.

A deep black spot on the life line with a star or cross on Saturn, shows sudden death or murder, and may be counted to occur where the spot on life line makes its appearance.

THE TRIANGLE.

(Diagram 27, No. 8.)

Is a good sign wherever located. It gives power, accuracy, diplomacy and aptitude for scientific pursuits. On the mount of Jupiter, successful diplomacy, denoting extraordinary success in the organization and handling of people.

On Saturn special talent for the mystical, mesmerism, aptitude for occult sciences, study of human magnetism.

On Apollo it denotes practical science. assisting art and a calm demeanor towards success and fame; celebrity will never spoil life.

On Mercury, restless qualities are checked, giving shrewdness in politics and learned professions; fortunate in business with scientific ability.

On Mars, military distinction, science in warfare, calmness in a crisis, presence of mind in danger.

On Luna, gives science and system in the development of ideas.

On Venus, prudence in soul, power of selfcontrol; it quiets the passionate desires on a good hand.

The spear and tripod are both fortunate and good signs for success, on whatever mount found.

THE CALCULATION OF DATES.

Events and time may be calculated on the life, head and heart lines, as marked on (Diagrams Nos. 4 and 28).

The life line commences from near the mount of Jupiter (side of the hand); likewise the heart and head lines.

On the lines of fate and fortune it is counted upwards, commencing near the wrist. The student should give a margin of fully twelve months as to events, yet often time may be predicted to six months, and even nearer than that. (Diagram No. 4) introduces the author's new method, while (Diagram No. 28) may be termed the general method of determining events.

Diagram No. 28.

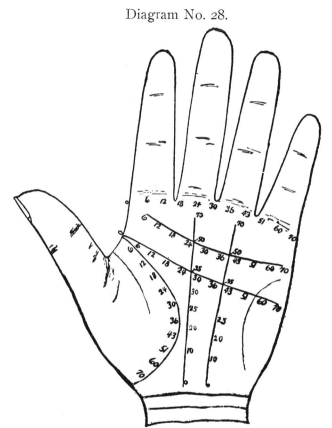

General System of Measurement.

LINES AND SIGNS ON FINGERS AND MOUNTS.

FINGER OF JUPITER.

A single line from root of finger to first phalange: nobility of character, great honours.

Many lines on the first phalange: ill health. The same with remaining fingers.

Transverse lines on second: ability to lie.

Star on second: sign of wickedness.

Cross on second: friendship with the great.

Star on third: an evil life.

Many lines from the mount across root to the third phalange: determination to succeed; a high spirit.

LINES ON THE MOUNT OF JUPITER.

A single line: success. Confused lines crossing the mount horizontally: persistent but unlucky efforts towards success.

Many lines crossing each other: immorality.

A grill: selfishness, ridiculous pride, a dominant spirit.

A triangle: good sense.

FINGER OF SATURN.

This finger much lined shows impulsiveness.
A single line traversing the whole finger shows folly.
A triangle shows occultism.
Star on first phalange shows a great but fatal event.
Cross on third phalange, no family.

ON THE MOUNT.

A single line, sign of luck and happiness in the end of life.

Numerous hair lines, a cut on the breast.
A cross, misfortune.
Ray lines across the mount, obstacles to success.
Star, danger of violent death.
A triangle, a talent for mystic science.

FINGER OF APOLLO.

A single line from root to first phalange shows destruction and fame.

Straight lines on third phalange, a happy existence.

Many lines rising from root of finger to first phalange, reverses due to women.

ON THE MOUNT.

A cross, ill luck in art or wealth.

A grill, boasting, scoffing and envy.

A star, riches obtained which bring trouble.

A triangle, sign of an architect.

FINGER OF MERCURY.

A single line from root to first phalange success in scientific research and literature; if more than one, failure.

A line from second to first phalange, good intelligence.

A cross on third phalange, shows theft.

A grill, cheating and dishonesty.

On the Mount of Mercury.

A single line on mount, a financial change for good.

Two or three deep lines, the study of chemistry and nursing aptitude. These lines on a woman's hand are an indication that she will marry a doctor.

Many lines on a woman's hand, she will be a chatter-box.

Numerous fine hair lines, wounds or sores on the legs.

A triangle, diplomacy; a good politician.

MOUNT OF VENUS.

Many lines, affectionate, but passionate; if crossed by others into a grill, the reverse.

Many lines passing down the mount to the palm, show ill-success in love.

A single line coming from this mount to plain of Mars, shows a very strong influence of some one from the other sex during the larger portion of life.

A mount without lines indicates coldness and sometimes a short life.

A single cross, shows a happy love affair or marriage.

MOUNT OF MARS.

Many lines on this mount make the native passionate and angry; liable to strike blows.

A cross if red, shows danger of suicide or murder.

Counting the lines on percussion of mount will numerate the subject's enemies; being broken or not, shows power of injury.

A grill indicates homicidal tendencies.

MOUNT OF LUNA.

Numerous lines on the percussion shows a worry; inclined to meet trouble half way; torments of anxiety.

Cross bars, sadness and discontent.

A triangle, wisdom of mysticism.

A star, hypocrisy, treason; a danger of drowning.

Squares give vigor and power to the organ on which they are found, except on Venus, where they indicate imprisonment or retiring from the world.

Suns indicate success and reputation.

Islands show hereditary disease; irregularity.

Triangles show science and talent.

PLANETARY SIGNS.

(Diagrams Nos. 4 and 23.)

Show the signs on the corresponding Mounts.

ON JUPITER.

Sign of ♃ (Jupiter), it will add to the quality of this mount, giving dignity of character.

Sign of ♄ (Saturn), gives taste and ability for occult science, with prudence.

Sign of ☉ (Sun), gives love of brilliant color, art and magnificence.

Sign of ☿ (Mercury), power of administration.

Sign of ♂ (Mars), shows genius in the command of military forces.

ON SATURN.

Sign of ♄ (Saturn), gives strong religious tendencies, love of the mysterious and philosophy.

Sign of ♃ (Jupiter), gives a desire for fame through discoveries in the above.

Sign of ☉ (Sun), gives beautiful expression of thought.

Sign of ☿ (Mercury), gives ability for astronomy, and the solving of mathematical problems.

Sign of ♀ (Venus), gives passion where opposite sex is concerned, hopelessness and despair.

Sign of ♂ (Mars), in religious debate is cruel and severe.

On Apollo.

Sign of ☉(Sun), shows genius in art, riches and distinction.

Sign of ♄ (Saturn), one who paints and depicts all that is sorrowful and saddening.

Sign of ♃ (Jupiter), gives elegance and distinction in art or wealth.

Sign of ☿ (Mercury), gives fine expression and success in literature, if the hand is otherwise good.

Sign of ♀ (Venus), idealism, a love of poetry.

Sign of ☽(Moon), with large mount of Moon, too much imagination in literary and artistic work.

On Mercury.

Sign of ☿ (Mercury), strengthens the good or bad qualities of the mount.

Sign of ♃ (Jupiter), on a bad hand, vanity; on good hand, success in science.

Sign of ♄ (Saturn), a sad, doleful nature, but clever.

Sign of ☉ (Sun), a philosopher.

Sign of ♀ (Venus), consideration for their loved one's future.

Sign of ☽ (Moon), a scheming erratic person.

Sign of ♂ (Mars), a violent thief.

On Venus.

Sign of ♃ (Jupiter), loves cajolery.

Sign of ♂ (Mars), unrestrained passion.

On Luna.

Sign of ☽ (Luna), somnambulism, imagination, diseased.

Sign of ♃ (Jupiter), dreams of riches unattainable.

Sign of ♄ (Saturn), superstitious.

Sign of ☿ (Mercury), speculation, ruinous.

Sign of ♀ (Venus), always longing for change and
new sensations.

Sign of ♂ (Mars), a sign of insanity with violence.

THE QUADRANGLE.

Is the horizontal elongated space stretching itself clear across the hand between the lines of heart and head. It includes the upper mount of Mars towards the percussion, i. e., if the quadrangle is not malformed by some abnormal development. (See Diagram No. 23.)

To be well formed it should be larger towards the percussion, not narrow in the center; the interior should not be traversed by too many lines.

When formed as described it will indicate a powerful intellect, broadmindedness, strong friendship, calm disposition, and an affectionate nature.

When narrow it indicates the ideas are narrow, it fails to see a point from another person's reasoning; there will be bigotry regarding religion and severe morality.

When very wide, it is abnormal and indicates ideas too broad for good, both religious and moral, carelessness of thought, and want of order in the brain.

When narrow, like a waist in the center, it indicates injustice and prejudice.

When very wide under Saturn and Jupiter and narrow near the percussion, it indicates the person will change generosity of views and broadness of mind to prejudice and bigotry.

When a star is found on any portion of the quadrangle, it must be taken as a good sign, especially under a favorable mount.

THE GREAT TRIANGLE.

Found in the centre of palm and formed by the life, head and liver lines. In case of no liver line, the fame or fate line should be taken from the third angle, but the mind will not be so broad and capable as when health line forms the third angle.

When this triangle is broad and well formed, it denotes breadth of views, a noble and generous nature.

When badly formed, with weak and wavy or broken lines, it shows a mean and cowardly spirit who will go with the majority and not upon principle.

UPPER ANGLE.

When the line of Sun forms its base, the individual will be strong and resolute but will have narrow views.

Formed by head and life lines, clear and pointed, the subject will be refined and delicate, sensitive of the feelings of others.

If very obtuse, a sign of stupidity, hasty bad temper, constantly giving offence, lacking application in study.

MIDDLE ANGLE.

Formed by the head and health or liver lines, if well formed and broad, it indicates keen intelligence, power of brain and capability for study. Also generally indicative of longevity.

If too heavy and broad, the subject is wanting in industry and kindness of heart.

If too sharp and pointed, it shows a nervous and irritable nature.

THE LOWER ANGLE.

Formed by life and health lines. When very acute, it is not a good sign, showing a weak constitution. It is good when slightly obtuse, indicating broad-mindedness and a generous spirit.

This angle may be formed by the conjunction of the fate and fortune lines.

If this angle is found to be defective or wanting in the hand of a child, he should not be pressed in his studies, but rather allowed to develop at his own pace.

THE BRACELETS OR RASCETTES.

The lines which encircle the wrist show length of life, each a period of about 27 years.

A royal bracelet consists of four lines. It is said the fortunate possessor will gain all this world can give.

The line close to the hand is the only really important one. This line when rising into the palm the shape of an arch, indicates weakness of the internal organs.

If the bracelets are well defined, uncrossed and deep, it shows a happy existence and a calm disposition, whether of short life or long life.

If the lines are near the palm, they denote more noble and elevated views than when lying low on the wrist, which is a sign of inferiority.

Chained lines show a laborious life, and continuing without breaking, success at last.

Branches on the bracelets signify distinction and honor.

If the lines are much broken and badly marked the result is trouble, distress, even disgrace.

Lines rising from the bracelets extending to Luna, show distant travel and voyages; if ending with a star, shipwreck; if in both, drowning.

If a line running to Jupiter, the subject will travel much, even around the world.

A line extending from the bracelets to mount of **Sun,** indicates a reputation gained through associating with persons of position, but if it first crosses to Luna, **turning** round the mount of Mars at the percussion of hand, it is a clear proof of misfortune, trials and tribulations, especially if irregular and broken.

Travel lines ending at life line show death on a journey; an angle at the centre of the rascette, money by inheritance or coming position.

DELINEATIONS OF A LADY'S HAND.

The hand print is that of an English lady, whom I met in America.

This is a pronounced specimen ot the broken head line, caused through heart grief.   The finger tips have not been given quite their correct shape by the artist, the true type being spatulate, with fingers and palm about equal in length, indicating self confidence and a desire for more than just sufficient, loving order, system and authority, with mechanical and artistic ability.

The description of left hand is necessary to show exactly the meaning of the broken head line in the right.

LEFT HAND.

Has heart line rising from centre of the mount Jupiter and continuing its course to the percussion under Mercury, showing firmness and strength in affections, the highest type of love, worship of the heart's ideal; such a line has few love affairs.

The line of head; a fine one rising well under the mount of Jupiter, slightly but distinctly separated from the line of life, indicating self confidence; it continues in a gradual slope until arriving at a point directly beneath the third and fourth fingers, where it takes a delicate curve upwards and stops on mount of Mars, this showing great

Diagram No. 29.

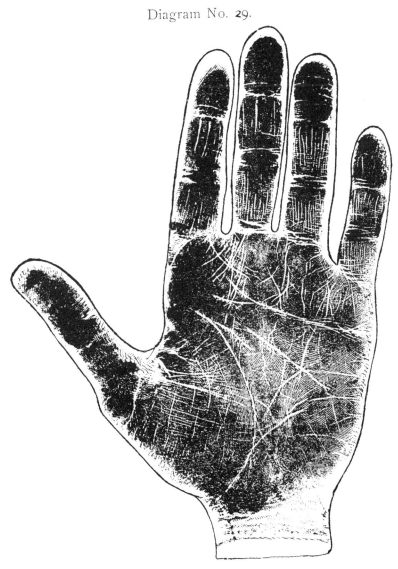

A Lady's Hand.

energy, talent and determination of purpose, very tolerant views, unusual ambition, combined with strong reasoning faculties.

The gradual slope in this line leads the native towards imaginative work, either painting, music, or mechanical invention; the gradual slope on Mars giving fine business discretion. She might have won unusual success in a business life.

The quadrangle shows a broad-minded disposition, being able to see things from a very sensible standpoint.

The line of life short, not reaching to more than the 50th year, indicates the father would die rather young anyway he must have died before his 60th year.

The fate line and other indications show loss through relatives in nearly all the parts of life that make up happiness; her love matters were met with rebuff and cruel interference from relatives, such as to give the greatest mental anguish to the native, which must have continued for some years, showing that the great affection indicated by the heart line, must have clung with great tenacity to its object, trying to hope against hope, for a time to arrive when love could be rewarded, but apparently the wishes of her tormentors were observed, though at great cost for as seen in the right hand impression the head line broke between 22 and 25 years and almost destroyed the mental balance. One portion of the head line joins to the life line, destroying confidence in self, the readiness of thought and promptness of action, hitherto having been strong characteristics, which might have led her on the way to a successful and happy life.

If she had married at 21, she would now have been in a successful and happy position in life.

The head line makes a new start from beneath the mount of Saturn, showing circumstances caused the loss of happiness, and this piece of the head line starting from the most unfortunate place, seems to make great effort to rectify matters. But the spirit and energy have been all but crushed out of life, the brightness and clearness of intellect gone, replaced by a longing to do something, but does not know what. The longing to leave it all came too late, the fatal card was thrown by hands that should have thrown the winner; the beauty and brightness of intellect gone, the heart almost broken (drooping branch from heart line), and still cannot tear herself from the love of some ideal, whom she had seen worthy. Pride not the cause, nor love of wealth, nor broken under Apollo or Mercury, neither have those who prevented her success in life been able to keep her and in these cases seldom desire. Crosses on Mars under Jupiter indicate she contemplated life worth living, but being surrounded by squares she was preserved from attempting any violence to herself.

The study of chemistry and nursing as an occupation would have been fairly successful; much aptitude is shown in the direction of art, but no fame.

Some good talent for invention or in home life, she certainly would distinguish herself as a dexterous and useful individual, as she is well domesticated.

The fate line not good, shows her judgment where her own happiness is concerned, is always wrong and mostly from a mistaken sense of duty.

The line of Mars percussion to cross on head line indicates an enemy, apparently a relative of military bearing, whose cruel severity brought great mental suffering.

In all her views and opinions she would be very generous, and greatly dislike squabbling over small matters. The disposition forgiving and would not harbor. revenge. No matter how the world tosses her about, some purity of spirit will be left.

She is unselfish in affection, but a certain intolerance for all but the right person, making marriage with any but the right man a most unhappy venture.

Death of a near relative is shown between 15 and 20.

About 19 or 20 appears to commence trouble in home life, concerning herself, which returns at different periods, more or less, until 27 or 28.

The best opportunity for happiness and position was between 20 and 25.

Little or no benefit from relatives.

No great success in fame or position.

Better to serve than be occupied in independent ventures.

THE STUDY HANDS.

The study hands presented here are prints from the hands of one of the most distinguished novelists of the day. But no name can be given in connection.

The nature is indicated as somewhat emotional and a good amount of impetuosity. Self control has in a great measure been acquired. As the prominent thumb, strong head line and Mars better developed in the right hand than the left.

This line of head indicates she might do nearly anything she chose, but artistic and literary work she is specially adapted for.

She would be much influenced by music, possibly more than she would admit; but music hath charms, and organ and vocal music would meet with her appreciation.

The nature is rather critical, better judged if the nails could be seen; analysis and keen observation are observed.

She would be inclined to act quickly, on the spur of the moment.

Imagination is fully developed, being brought well into use; this is seen by the line of head curving in the upper part of mount of Moon; this also is well developed.

She is very energetic, but work is done by sudden impulse or inspiration, however, her best work is done during the fitful spells or moments.

What real hard work is done, comes more from a sense

Diagram No. 30.

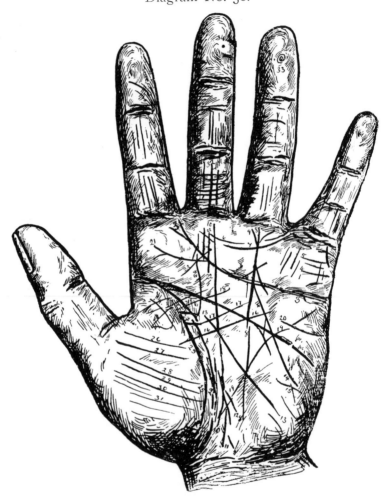

THE HAND OF A CELEBRATED AUTHOR.

Diagram No. 31.

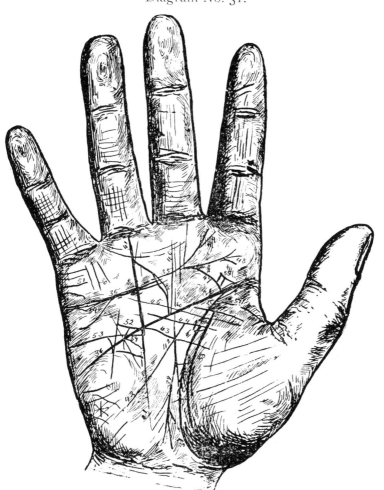

THE HAND OF A CELEBRATED AUTHOR

of duty, intellect combined with determination, as shown by head line and strong thumb.

Law and authority where it concerns herself she has no respect for, as she dearly loves freedom, being independent in both thought and action, shown by the position of first and second fingers and third and fourth.

Great mental power is shown by the head line; she is intensely human, very sympathetic and original in her work.

She studies human nature for the love of it, and is an excellent judge of character.

During the execution of her work, she possesses the power to throw herself entirely into another place, feeling and acting as she might in different circumstances; this will be very easily observed in her work.

In her affections she is passionate and warm hearted, a true friend, and would make a most devoted wife, but it must be under certain circumstances, for her likes and dislikes are strong; manliness and dignity of character is a necessity to such a nature; would we had more such women and fewer men of the type these women shun, for as is often the case, there shows tendency for ill fortune in love affairs.

There are some things and some people she would find it impossible to tolerate, being very sensitive and of nervous temperament and very susceptible to the influence of her surroundings; weather and general environment affect her strongly.

The health is good and she possesses strong vitality, the vital forces quickly renewed by line of Mars, visible in both hands. This has proved its worth and will assist her through severe sickness.

There is one troublesome sickness about the 24th or 25th year; the heart and chest or lungs seem to have been affected, no doubt rheumatic fever with its after complications. Some care will be needed again about the age of forty or forty-two; the line weakens and shows loss of vitality.

It is interesting to notice the square or preservation on the life line round the break at the time of the illness.

The long heart line running on to Jupiter indicates unselfishness in love, but also incapability for her to realize happiness unless the right person, especially in marriage.

She is not fond of too much detail, very generous in her views and opinions, very broad-minded; a lover of harmony and peace; would detest gossip or anything mean, trivial or underhanded.

She would not show revenge or malice; the temper is quick but soon over and very forgiving.

The line of fate indicates about the age of thirty a new start in life, seeming to arise from some strong intention of her own about that date; this continues and is most noticeable in the right hand.

The long line of influence, which rises from Luna, crossing the fate line, then ends and is cut across by two deep lines, about the same time the illness is marked.

These may have had something to do with the illness, as they show worry and interference.

It is likely that this lady's life has been threatened, as the line from Mars to a star on the head line generally shows the work of an enemy, may be seen also on the left hand; but this is also surrounded by the mark of preservation, the square.

The mark again occurs on mount of Moon in right hand, star surrounded by square, showing danger from water. Several journeys and voyages being indicated.

She shows great sympathy with dramatic art; had the sun finger been more spatulate she would have no doubt taken up this as a profession.

Some interest in medical science is shown.

The fame line in left hand shows a splendid chance of fame and wealth, though it is rather cut through and interfered with in both hands; there is still every chance of distinction in the chosen path, being well marked upon the Sun finger.

SOME DEDUCTIONS AND RESULTS FROM COMBINATIONS OF PROMINENT SIGNS.

When the line of head extends to the side of the mount of Moon, this shows investigations with conclusions devoid of reason, ineffectual groping in the dark after knowledge.

Young people should be guarded from such people as advisers; the tendency is that they would lead their minds astray.

When line of head curves towards the line of heart and ends there, the indication is the reason is controlled by the love and passions.

When the head line starts from the outside of hand under Jupiter, and makes a sudden curve towards heart line under Saturn, afterwards continuing its course in a normal direction, it denotes fatal affections; nought but trouble may be expected from them. If the line after going up towards Saturn takes a very sloping course low on the mount of Moon, the subject will first be made very unhappy, and in all probability become insane. When the line of head is forked, one branch going to the Moon and the other to Mercury, the mount of Mercury being largely developed and Jupiter mount flat, the person will be a great hypocrite, selfish and cunning.

When the line of head rises well on Jupiter, which is

well developed, then, passes near the line of life almost
touching it, continuing with a gradual slope nearly across
the hand, when a small but graceful curve stops on Mars
(percussion), and Mercury is developed on the percusssion,
this denotes a fine business capability.

When the fate line is well developed, such a person
will be very successful in a business life.

When the fate line has two branches, one from the
Moon and another from Venus, and then itself goes
right up the hand to its own mount, it denotes fearful
struggles with the passions and imagination or caprice,
but success in the end. If the mounts of Moon and Venus
be large, the strife is keener.

When the lines of life, head and heart are strongly
marked with a well developed Venus and poorly developed
Jupiter and all join together under Jupiter, this is a fatal
sign, as there is nothing such a person would not do to
gratify his passions, being headstrong and blind to danger.
Such a person is always in peril and may die suddenly.

A line starting from Mars (percussion), and taking its
course to the Sun mount, signifies a desire for fame and
distinction, and no price is too dear for the gratification of
that wish, even if violence has to be resorted to; they will
bring themselves to the front.

With Venus and Mercury fully developed and a strong
and direct line apparently tie the two together, is indicative of some habit gaining the mastery over the subject
and dishonest means will be used to gratify it if necessary.

When the hands are soft, fingers pointed, line of head

short and low mount of Jupiter, this shows absolute idle-ness and selfishness, mischief is their playmate.

Long, square fingers are never satisfied when the first phalange of thumb is long, the second being undeveloped these are unreasonable tyrants.

When the thumb with long, stiff and thin fingers turns inwards, the hand narrow, no mount of Luna, this indi-cates cruelty with tyranny; these kind of people will starve and ill-use children to the death and will abuse and mal-treat almost any creature they have the control of.

When fingers are short, thick and hard, the mount of Mars lined, low mount of Moon, the line of life long, deep and red, the whole aspect of the hand having a clumsy ap-pearance, these are the signs of a brutal nature; such peo-ple have no understanding of the word sympathy, and like the tiger, love to torment their prey.

The third phalange of the fourth finger, long and thick with large Mercury and Moon mounts are indica-tions of the liar.

High mount of Venus with thick third phalanges of all the fingers indicates greediness.

A short heart line, very long line of head, hard hand, with the fingers very close together and thumb stiff, long third phalange of second finger, show a nature full of avarice. These are the people who sell a thing and then grieve they did not ask for more. Short, square nails, with high mount of Mars under Jupiter, and deep red lines, in-dicate a person with little control over their temper.

Long, smooth fingers, long line of head, Mercury well

developed, and long fourth finger make the orator who moves the people with eloquence and fluency of speech.

When the hand is firm, both mounts of Mars well developed, and straight fingers, the palm being larger at the basement, having a tapering appearance, it indicates a very courageous person, who is always prepared to meet obstacles, and though he may fight to win, finds a way of showing his generous spirit.

Such an individual will carry a pleasant, open countenance, his step is firm but elastic, and if the hand contains a good head and fate line, his chances are great for success in a military career. But it must be remembered that a well developed mount of Jupiter and first finger is a necessity, for otherwise he will be vulgar, undignified and wanting in controlling power.

When the hand is hard, with long fingers, except the first, which is weak and twisted, the third finger being nearly as long as the second, the head and life lines much joined, a long third phalange to second finger, long first phalange to thumb, this denotes a want of dignity of character; such a person has abilities and desire for fame and wealth. A man with such a hand gains his ends by most undignified and discreditable means; he is impatient of the routine of work and study and very selfish, consequently will grasp the work of any person and call it his own, if it will help him to the praise of the multitude; he has no scruples and sees no need of a dignified course, so long as he obtains what he wants, it does not matter how; his manner is submissive until a grip is obtained, then smiles with a grin of satisfaction on the loser.

When the hand is large, the fingers long and a long head line, it denotes great love of detail; such a person is a stickler for etiquette, and will be easily put out or annoyed by trifles, the writing will generally be small, and they have an eye to the finish of a piece of work and will spend a great amount of time in working out a problem, especially if these hands are knotted, there is a quality of perseverance that gives tenacity in the execution of a plan or problem once taken hold of.

A love of order is shown by developed joints or what is termed knots, knot of philosophy order in ideas (between the second and third phalange), knot between the second and third phalange, gives order in material things, to do with management.

Imagination is shown by long, conic-shaped fingers and a high mount of Luna, and drooping head line.

When the thumb is strong with first phalange well developed, long, clear line of heart forked on Jupiter.

Long line of head, this shows constancy in affections.

When the hand is much lined, with white spots on the nails, the fingers having a bend backwards, often spatulate in shape, it indicates nervousness, but not necessarily want of courage.

When the thumb is turned out, with a well developed mount of Jupiter and a long line of heart taking its rise from that mount, it denotes generosity; such will help their fellow men with money, sympathy or influence.

When the fortune line is long and uncrossed, a well developed mount of Mercury, with one clear line on it, and upward branches from life line, it indicates money obtained through a business career.

Money from inheritance or legacy is shown by a cross or angle from the first line; if a star is near the inheritance will be large. Also by two horizontal lines on the first phalange of the first finger.

When the fate line is long and clear, ending on the mount of Saturn and branch lines from head to Jupiter, this denotes money from appointments.

If the fate line starts from mount of Moon, much depends on the influence of others; spatulate fingers, a large mount of Apollo, with widely separated lines of life and head. A poorly developed mount of Apollo with a star on it, indicates riches obtained; but fatal to happiness.

A long, sloping line of head, with the third finger nearly as long as the second and the thumb bending back, indicates the gambler.

When a branch line rises from head line to mount of Mercury, it denotes commercial gain.

When the hand is extreme spatulate in formation, with large mount of Mercury and cross there, it indicates a very dishonest character, who will be persistently on the alert for petty actions of theft.

Well developed mount of Mercury with third or fourth vertical lines near the percussion, show ability for chemistry. A long third finger, square and long second phalange of fourth finger, shows aptitude for business.

A line of intuition with an island near the end, a drooping head line terminating in a fork on mount Luna, is a sure indication of clairvoyance. Such people make rapid thought readers.

A long first finger and long, straight line of head, indicates economy.

A very hollow palm denotes failure in money matters and the general affairs of life.

When the first finger is long and straight, with a well developed mount of Jupiter, high mounts of Moon and Venus, well developed mount of Mercury, with long, pointed fourth finger, it indicates the qualifications for the church.

If the fingers have both knots and a strong thumb, it gives the strength of the clergy resistance, reason and union, being great power of argument; but if the fingers are pointed and knotted, and the second phalange of thumb long, faith and reason will be in continual conflict; with spatulate finger tips, he will preach some new doctrine and will be quite positive in his delivery and very demonstrative.

When the fingers are long, smooth and pointed, he will be very enthusiastic, love a beautiful service, a lover of art and dogmatic.

Musical talent is shown by a line of head drooping on to the mount of Luna, well developed, also Venus full, good line of fortune and high mount of Saturn and Apollo, with supple fingers; Apollo and Venus represent melody; Saturn and Moon, harmony.

Square and knotted fingers are good for composers.

A good doctor will have the following indications: Large mount of Mercury, with vertical lines on the face of mount near percussion for chemistry, good mounts of Mars for surgery, large mount of Moon for diagnosis, long, deep line of head and well formed thumb.

A good lawyer will have the following indications: A long straight fourth finger, rising well above the first phalange of third finger, with good mount of Mercury, the thumb supple and long second phalange, good line of fate and fortune, with a clear, well-marked line of head.

INDICATIONS AND SIGNS.

Simplified in short order as found in the human hand.

Accidents (are indicated) by a line falling downward from an island on Saturn, attacking life line. When ending with a cross or life line there will be a narrow escape.

An influence line from mount Venus crossing life line to the mount of Saturn.

Stars in the plain of Mars and crosses on mount Saturn gives accidents. They are serious when the head line is crossed under mount of Sun.

Activity—Is indicated by an elastic hand with a long head line, a palm shorter than fingers with square tips, a well developed first phalange of thumb with a good mount of Mars and Mercury.

Actors should have fingers longer than palm, conical tips, except finger of Sun, which may be spatulate, and the finger and mount well developed with a head line forked at the end.

Ambition is indicated by a good mount and finger of Jupiter, a well proportioned hand, the life line commencing from Jupiter or a branch from life line on the mount, a line running along the finger from base to tip, a good line of fate, likewise that of the liver, a good mount of Sun, Mercury and Mars all tend to ambition.

Amorousness—A much raised mount of Venus with distinct ring of Venus, a drooping head line, full developed mount of Luna, a heart line commencing from mount of Saturn.

Anger—Excessively developed mount of Mars, a good heart line and mount of Venus, nails well shaped, pink on the outer edges.

Animals (a love for)—Strong mount of Venus and Sun, with a defined heart line; first phalange of fingers in proportion, short.

Apoplexy—An uneven liver line, red where it crosses heart line; long and red blotches on heart line, very red skin, hollow plain of Mars, excessive mount of Jupiter, often lined; a grill and star on mount Luna.

Architecture—A good head line, square-tipped fingers, sometimes slightly spatulate; long, square nails and second phalange of thumb. A good mount of Sun and Venus for art. Mount Mercury for calculation.

Art—The fingers should be conical for painting and square for sculpture and science; the mount of Sun and Venus fully developed and for imaginative work, good mount of Luna, with sloping head line. The line of fate in all cases is good when termination on mount Apollo or a branch from head line to that mount. The line of the Sun is also a good sign to start from life line.

Asthma—A badly traced liver line with quadrangle narrow and a black spot under that angle.

Avarice—A thin, hard hand with fingers bent forward, narrow quadrangle, the line of head crossing from side to side of hand, thumb bent forward, mounts generally dried up, heart line often terminating on Mercury.

Benevolence—Long, brittle nails, a good mount of Venus and Jupiter, wide quadrangle; a good heart line commencing with a fork from Jupiter.

Biliousness—Palm yellow, cold and clammy, indirect liver line.

Blindness—A cross on upper part of liver line and a circle on heart line.

A circle on life line. Two circles refers to both eyes. A star in triangle close to liver line.

Breast (Wound)—Capillary cross lines on mount Saturn.

Brain Troubles—A pale and wide line of head with black spots on it or broken; a crossed or blurred head line, much rayed or broken chainlike, plain of Mars hollow towards head, an influence line from head to mount Venus, with a star at the end next head line; a wavy head line.

Brilliancy is indicated by the line of Sun.

Broadmindedness—A well proportioned hand, square fingers, a good shaped quadrangle; long head line with prominent mount of Jupiter and Venus. Head line slightly separated from life line.

Business Hand—A line branching from head line to a good mount of Mercury; a fair line of fate and Sun; fingers square, rather longer than the palm with second knot; fourth finger well developed and a good liver line. Elastic palm; head line straight or half straight and remainder slightly sloping.

Chemistry is indicated by a good mount of Saturn and second finger; long knotted fingers, hands medium thickness.

Children (Death)—Interferences of the line by stars, dots, islands and bars.

Childbearing (Difficulties)—The life line closely

placed towards second phalange of the thumb; a line extending from mount Venus to mount Saturn. The first bracelet convex.

Clairvoyance—A soft hand with the mount of Luna, Saturn and Mercury well developed; many cross lines and a drooping head line, small thumb, a well formed intuition line and liver line. Often islands at the start and a poor heart line.

Concentration—A good thumb with knotted long fingers. The passive mount of Mars, Mercury and Jupiter well developed; small mount of Luna with a good head line.

Constancy—The passive mount of Mars with first phalange of thumb well developed. A straight and long line of head with heart line commencing, forked on Jupiter, with many small bracelet lines. Medium mount of Venus, few worry lines and small mount of the Moon.

Consumption—Many islands on head or liver line; life line weak and interrupted. Long knotted fingers, a thin palm, nails brittle, long, convex and fluted; excessive mount of Jupiter or that mount much lined.

Courage—Firm palm, fingers fairly long, a good mount of Jupiter and Venus; the lines of a good color with a well developed thumb, a heart line commencing from well marked and well up on Jupiter, with head line straight and clear. Full plain of Mars and mounts well developed.

Cowardice (respecting females)—A thick and soft hand without any hair; a small mount of Mars and Jupiter, nails narrow, thin and long, fingers bent forward, excessive mount of the Moon, Mercury and Saturn, with small triangle.

Critic, short nails, soft palms with second phalange of fingers and thumb excessive, a good mount of Mercury, first knot often a cross in plain of Mars.

Cruelty, small palm with long thin fingers, poor mount of Mars and Venus, heart line almost absent, Mercury and Sun excessive or badly lined, often a poor liver line and narrow quadrangle, drooping head line and women with hairy hands.

Deafness, islands and dots on head line under Saturn, exaggerated or much lined, and a big bulb like Venus.

Detail (a love of), long fingers, a good long head line, moderate mount of Luna, long second phalange of thumb, a good mount of Jupiter and Mercury.

Disappointed love, heart line barred, crossed with a branch from fate, also lines from Venus or life, cutting heart line, numerous downward branches from line of heart.

Discoverers, a strong, hard palm, with long third finger, large mount of Sun, Moon, Jupiter and Mars, spatulate fingers, longer than palm, head line often a little sloping.

Divorce, a line from Venus cutting an upward branch from life line, terminating on Mercury, often cutting the marriage line, also an influence line from Venus, extending to heart line forked.

Drowning, is signified by a star, on a voyage line from percussion of hand, cross line uneven, first phalange of all fingers, a line running from inside bracelet ending with a star on Luna.

Eloquence, high mount of Mercury with a long fourth finger, long head line sloping towards Luna and long smooth fingers, line of life and head slightly separated.

Engineering (ability for), long spatulate, knotted fingers with a large hand, the finger of Saturn and mount of Mars, extra developed with a good straight head line, and scientific marks on Mercury.

Engagement (broken), a broken heart line under mount Saturn, through fate.

Extravagance, the thumb supple and set low down fingers flexible, a sloping head line, a poorly marked line and mount of Sun, with the fate line only visible during early life.

Fainting fits, line of liver, connected at the commencement with life, a heart line chained, curving towards head line.

Fame, a clear line of fate from bracelet to mount Saturn, Sun or Jupiter, sister lines with the Sun line on a good mount, a good head line as well as that of the heart, a star on Jupiter and star at the end of a line of the Sun.

Female troubles, lower part of mount Luna excessive and much lined, with a cross on mount, the life line during the middle part shooting out towards mount of Moon, and a hollow plain of Mars near the Moon.

Fever, skin dry, life line dotted with red, the lines often red.

Fortune, is indicated by the line of fate and Sun, commencing from under a well formed triangle; the first phalange of the thumb should be long with a good head line, long and fine mount of Sun, as well as that of Mercury and Mars, a fate line may often branch on Sun or Mercury.

Frivolity, a short finger of Saturn, pointed, a poor head line and small first phalange of thumb, a very small passive mount of Mars and broken-up Sun line.

Gambler, short smooth fingers on a soft hand, the finger of Sun as long or nearly as the second, sometimes longer, a drooping head line, supple thumb and large mount of Luna.

Generosity, a wide space between first finger and the thumb.

Guilty (attachments), an island on heart, fate line or marriage line, an influence line from Venus to life, with an island thereon, or an island on mount Venus.

Headache, a chained, short head line, liver line wavy and red at termination, head line cut or crossed with small lines.

Heart trouble, short square bluish nails, an influence line cutting heart line from Venus, heart line chained, blurred, broken or barred, hollow plain of Mars towards heart.

Hysteria, a ring of Venus, unbroken or with cross bars, sometimes a double line is found, a finger of Saturn ill formed, a star on Luna, connected by an influence line to Venus.

Ill health, a palm, with thin lines poorly marked, lacking color, the life and head lines broken, chained and linked, dots on main lines, liver connected with life.

Imagination (diseased), indications—An excessive

mount of Moon, forked line of head, drooping with girdle of Venus, with a soft hand thin and transparent.

Inconstancy, a small first phalange of thumb, short head line and chained heart line; the hand soft, fingers smooth, conical tips, lower mount of Mars with a cross and a circle inside the third angle of the triangle.

Indigestion (chronic), an island in life line, the head line badly traced with a wavy line of the liver.

Insanity, a sloping head line to the mount of Moon, with many confused lines thereon, the sign of the Moon on mount Saturn, a wavy head line chained or blurred, rising close to heart line under mount of Sun or Mercury, line of head merging into liver line with a forked life line at commencement, head line often split.

Intuition, short, conical fingers and nails, the hands thin and soft, a good mount of Mercury and Moon, first phalange of fingers smooth and above the average length, a clear line of intuition, a line of fate rising from Luna, a drooping head line with triangle on the Moon.

Kidney disease, a long voyage line reaching almost to life, forked at the end, the lower part of mount Luna excessive or much lined, often a cross on flat mount.

Lawyer, a large mount of Mars or Mercury with a head line separated from life at commencement, forked at the termination, a long little finger and second phalange of the thumb.

Laziness, a soft thick, flabby hand, short conical fingers, overdeveloped mounts of Sun, Moon and Venus, head line drooping with short first phalange of the thumb.

Liar, a drooping head line forked at termination, the

absence of mount Jupiter, crooked little finger, with excessive mount of Mercury and Moon, grilled or crossed.

Literature, a prominent mount of Moon, Sun, Venus and Mercury, head line drooping and forked at end, conical fourth finger with a long first phalange, a line extending from bracelet across to mount of the Sun, the hands large, star on Mercury.

Liver disease, a clammy, cold, damp hand, the lines of yellowish color, especially the liver line which is irregular and broken, excessive mount of Mercury, much lined and dark spots on Luna.

Losses (financial), the fate line with an island, the same on the liver line, a hollow plain of Mars, the Sun line broken, barred or with islands and stars.

Mathematicians, a good finger and mount of Mercury, second phalange of fingers above average, the thumb long with a straight head line and small mount of Luna and Sun, the palm hard and the fingers long and knotted.

Memory, a very good straight head line, likewise liver with the finger of Jupiter and Mercury conical.

Morbidness, the finger of Saturn and first phalange excessively long, the mount abnormal, with confused lines, a drooping head line towards mount Luna, liver line wavy, palm soft, of a yellow tinge, lines weak.

Murder, the head line rising high up the hand to that of heart, sometimes surpassing it, mount Saturn excessive or much rayed, excessive mount of Sun, Mercury, with many cross lines, a thin hand, knotted fingers, mount Luna much crossed and grilled.

Music, long second finger, good high mount of Saturn, line of fortune, line of head descending on Luna, supple fingers for performers, square knotted for composers, high mount Saturn and Luna for harmony, high Apollo and Venus for melody, thick and hard with spatulate fingers and a club thumb, and a short head and heart line.

Music, the Sun, Moon and Venus well developed, the head line drooping, the hand impressionable, with conic smooth fingers.

Nervousness, the hand much crossed, a large mount of Moon and Saturn much lined, spots or dots on Luna, life line linked or irregular, a flat end of the thumb, plain of Mars hollow near Luna.

Neuralgia, many dots on headline, with sometimes an island, deep colorless indentations.

Painting, long line of head, supple fingers short square second, and all the first phalanges long.

Paralysis, an excessive mount of Saturn with a star thereon, main lines poorly marked, a grill or star on Luna, short nails of a triangular shape.

Passion or anger, a palm thick and hard, the skin red and nails short and broad, the bottom overrun by flesh, excessive mount and plain of Mars, a deeply colored Mars line and red skin, hair generally on all phalanges.

Physician, an elastic hand, fingers long, knotted and square with the medical sign on Mercury.

Poetry, finger of Jupiter long and pointed with high mount, good mount of Luna and Venus, head line descending on Luna, heart line turning high on Jupiter.

Pride, a grill on mount Jupiter, lines running from life line or head, high up on Jupiter, an excessive mount of Jupiter and Sun, plain of Mars well developed, in fact all mounts.

Religion, a good mount of Jupiter, flexible palm smooth pointed fingers.

Selfishness, fingers thick at base, hands hard, thick and flabby, the lines and palms pale colored, mount Venus excessively developed, a poor heart line and many branches downwards.

Somnambulism, the line of intuition well marked, commencing with an island, the liver line running close to percussion, with an island at the commencement.

Spendthrift, the finger of Sun and mount excessively developed, the thumb supple, high mount of Moon and Jupiter, head and life lines separated.

Suicidal tendencies, hand generally long, sloping head line, developed mount of Luna towards base, line of head very much connected with life line and well developed mount of Saturn.

PROPENSITIES FOR MURDER.

First class of hand, ungovernable temper and brute passion on the elementary hand or similar line of head short, thick and red, nails short and red, hand very heavy and coarse, thumb set very low down on hand, short and thick second phalange, first phalange clubbed very short and broad and square, mount of Venus abnormally large, with ungovernable temper.

Second class of hand, line of head heavily marked, growing upwards in an abnormal position, rising high towards Mercury, and before it reaches that place it completely leaves its place on right hand and enters the heart line.

Hand usually hard, thumb not abnormally thick but long, very stiff, contracting inward.

Third type of hand, the leading features very thin. Hand hard, long; fingers slightly curved inward; thumb long, both phalanges well developed, rarely bent or inclining outward; line of head may not be out of proper place but set higher than usual across the hand and very long and thin.

Venus may be high or low. When low, the person may commit crime for the simple sake of it; when high, more for the sake of gratifying animal desires. Such a hand will rarely kill by violence, poison being its chief instrument, administered with skill.

Superstitious:- a very drooping head line towards Luna; that mount excessively developed; the finger of Saturn and its mount abnormal in some way.

Teacher:- long, knotted, square fingers; a good thumb and mount of Mars, Mercury, Sun and Venus; a good little finger; the head line slightly separated from life line.

Toothache and neuralgia:- excessive mount of Saturn; liver and fate lines much interrupted and uneven; the second phalange of all fingers excessive.

Thief:- excessive mount of Mercury, with crooked finger on the elementary hand; few lines; mount of Jupiter absent; mount of Moon bulging out.

Timidity:- long knotted fingers which are bent inwards; a poor mount of Jupiter, Mars and Mercury; the head and life lines much pointed together at commencement, palm thin and soft.

Voyages are denoted by the heavy lines on face of mount Luna and the little hair lines which leave the life travelling on by life line side.

This indication is similar to the line of life dividing in the hand, if one branch goes around Venus and the other proceeding to base of the mount of Luna, it foretells that the native will make some great change from his native land to another.

The lines on Luna are of less importance, which show minor travels and changes.

The lines from the rascette or first bracelet rising into Mount of Luna are also more important than these on Luna. When the line of fate shows a beneficial change at some period, then these lines are beneficial and fortunate, and if the fate line does not show gain, the subject will make no advantageous removal.

When a line shows a journey extending from the first bracelet ending with a cross, the end of journey will be disappointment.

When the travel line ends with a square it shows danger through the journey, but the subject will be protected.

When the line ends with an island, the journey will result in loss.

The ascending lines from the rascette to Luna are not beneficial.

When the line crosses the hand and enters the mount of Jupiter, great positon and power will be gained and the journey very long.

If it runs to Saturn, some fatality will govern it. If to the Sun, it is most favorable and promises riches and celebrity. Running to Mercury, sudden and unexpected wealth will arise from it.

Horizontal lines on Luna, crossing the face of mount, reaching fate line, the journey will be long and important, and if they ascend by side of fate line they show travels that materially benefit the person.

If the end of these horizontal lines droop or curve downwards, it will be unfortunate; if they rise again, good.

When one of these lines crosses another, such a journey will be repeated for some important reason.

A square on such a line shows danger, but protection from accident and misfortune.

If the travel line runs into the line of head, causing a spot, island or break, it shows danger to the head, or accident arising from the journey.

The Daughter of the Sea.
Showing Parts of the Body ruled by the Planets.

MOTHER SHIPTON'S OMENS.

Which are said by the Ancients to exist in every day life.

Every person will be found in some measure skeptical about signs and warnings when a serious calamity is about to take place. Admonitions and forewarnings have been received; many such instances are on record; some warnings being followed by events of a pleasant character, others of a painful nature to the recipient. The belief in auguries and signs has been cherished by mankind ever since man was created.

The following are a few of the signs recognized by mankind as warnings at different stages of his existence:

A newly-married couple must possess an old chair, when first going into housekeeping, to bring good luck.

If you twirl a chair on one leg, you are turning friends from you.

If a chair breaks down upon which you are sitting, it indicates evil tidings.

When moving furniture, if some falls off a load, expect losses or sickness in the family.

An itching at the back of the neck signifies that either yourself or some one related to you will soon suffer a violent death.

If the palm of the right hand itches, you will soon receive some money.

If your right shoulder itches you will profit by a legacy, which is then being bequeathed to you.

If your palm of left hand itches, you are about to pay out some money.

If your left shoulder itches, you are about to bear a burden.

Should your right elbow itch, you will hear some pleasant news.

If your left, you will have a disappointment.

If your back itch, you are going to make a change.

If the knees or thighs, it also means a change in life.

If your right foot itch, you are going to take a journey, which will give you happiness.

If your left foot, you will take a journey, in which you will have some unpleasantness.

If your ankle itch, you will have an increase of domestic pleasures.

Fortune will accompany you through the day if you put your right shoe on first in the morning; but everything will go by the rule of contrary all through the day if you put the left shoe on first.

It is considered very unlucky to pass under a ladder or upon a grating in the pathway.

If on awakening first thing in the morning you see a dog or cat, a bird or a man pass to your right, it denotes a fortunate day.

To awake on your right side is most lucky, and get out on the right side of the bed.

To sneeze in the morning means misfortune is at hand, but in the afternoon, luck is coming to you soon.

When the right eye itches, you are going to see a friend; if the left, an enemy.

If the nose seems seized with a troublesome itching, you will either be kissed, cursed or vexed, or shake hands with a fool.

Some one is speaking ill of you if your lips itch.

Sneeze on Monday, sneeze for a kiss.

Sneeze on Tuesday, it is for a wish.

Sneeze on Wednesday, it is for gain.

Sneeze on Thursday, expect some pain.

Sneeze on Friday, sneeze for sorrow.

Sneeze on Saturday, see your true love tomorrow.

A buzzing or ringing in your right ear is the forerunner of pleasant news.

A ringing in your left ear, some unpleasant intelligence is about to be yours.

If you retire to rest without clearing the table, the youngest will get no sleep.

It is a sign of company if you forget to put coffee or tea in the pot.

If your apron string comes untied, somebody is speaking of you.

If you sing while making bread, you will cry before eating it.

When bread, cake or pie will burn in spite of your efforts to prevent it, your husband or lover is angry.

If in your tea several stalks float, on stirring it, they keep to the middle of the cup, you are going to talk to an absent friend; if on holding the spoon upright and still one or more cling to the spoon, you are soon to be married

If a dog howls at night, especially if it be midnight, it is a token of either death or sickness in your near vicinity.

The horse shoe is a lucky thing to keep, hang it over your doorway; from time immemorial it has been considered lucky to find a horse shoe, as it would protect a person from ill-luck.

Protection from drowning is the possession of a caul. Many sailors give large prices for these.

If the rats leave a ship before she sailed from port, it signifies she is going to sink; oftentimes sailors have refused to sail on a ship which the rats have left.

Drop a letter after it is sealed and any request it contains you will be denied.

If a watch fall out of your pocket or a stone out of your ring, it signifies sickness or death.

If a picture falls out of its frame, it is a sure sign of serious trouble or death.

To remove your wedding ring from your finger is very unlucky, or removing a ring long worn.

It is unlucky to destroy spiders.

If your cock crow in the hen roost three times at midnight, it is a sure sign of death in the family.

Washing in the same basin of water with another person will generally produce a quarrel.

If a bat flutter against your window pane, it signifies a death.

To hear an owl screech at night is very unlucky.

When parts of your body has sudden and shooting pains, some bad news is on the way to you.

To be called back is unlucky; to break the spell sit down a while.

You should step out of doors in the morning with the right foot first, this is lucky.

If you sing or whistle before breakfast, you will cry before supper.

It is unlucky to brush or comb the hair after sunset.

When a dog howls under a sleeper's window, that person will be very sick or die.

It is a bad sign to cross the path of a funeral procession, it indicates a death of some friend or relaitve soon.

If thirteen persons sit down to eat or drink, within a year one will die.

It is a sign of disappointment to sing while eating.

A married couple will not become rich until their wedding clothes are worn out.

Lovers should not present a sharp instrument to each other, it cuts love and is unlucky.

To break a looking-glass is very unlucky and signifies death.

It is very fortunate to have a cricket on the hearth.

To speak a rhyme involuntarily is lucky, and before speaking again wish and it will be granted.

To remove a cat when changing a residence is unfortunate, but if the cat follows of her own free will it shows good luck.

Never kill a cricket; it is unlucky.

To postpone a marriage is unlucky. At the time of a wedding it is very unlucky to put the bride's new boots on the table.

If a vacant chair is turned with great energy or rocked violently, the next person to sit in it will be sick within a year.

To drop a dishcloth is a preliminary to the arrival of company.

If a child born have thick, heavy hair it will die rich.

It is unlucky for a child to see itself in a mirror before it is twelve months old.

If a baby is fed with a silver or gold spoon, it will become wealthy.

Howling of dogs at any time is very unfortunate.

One, three, five, seven, nine and eleven, are lucky numbers, but thirteen is a very unlucky number.

There is a change in every person's fortune every seven years.

If your shoe string comes untied, your lover will play you false.

If you help a person to salt at table during meals, you will help them to sorrow.

Spilling salt foretells quarrels and strife.

Common salutes are always odd in number.

It is lucky to see a star shoot.

To have money in your pocket when you see the new moon over your right shoulder is very lucky.

When you see the first spring lamb in the field, if it be standing with its face toward you, turn your money over, for you will have luck that year.

But if its back be towards you, judge the contrary.

For an orphan child to come in the house is very lucky.

Rain drops on a young baby will give it freckles.

Never show a child's clothes to friends before it is born, for it is very unfortunate.

It is most unlucky for a young married woman to try on her mother's widow weeds or bonnet before having been first worn by the mother, for she, too, will be a widow before a year is out.

A new-born babe should remain in bed with its mother 24 hours, or it will not live to be old.

Wrap a new-born baby in borrowed or old clothes if you desire it to be fortunate.

No person can have more than seven years of ill-luck.

It is considered very unfortunate for a bettor to be spoken to during a horse race.

To whistle on the water increases the wind.

To have a spider's web stick to you is lucky.

It is very unlucky to cross knives.

It is unlucky to find a knife or any sharp instrument.

It is lucky to see a star shoot.

White spots on the nails are lucky.

Black spots are unlucky.

Yellow spots mean death.

To get up and turn your chair around will change your luck at cards or games of chance.

It is unlucky to sit against the grain of wood on the table while playing cards.

Always sit with the grain running toward you for luck.

To enter a house by one door and leave by another is very unfortunate.

It is not lucky to see the new moon through a glass.

For a woman to receive a pair of garters from a man is good.

It is not lucky to meet a widow when starting a journey, but is very fortunate to meet one at the end.

It is very unlucky to refuse any request of a widow.

To put any garment on the wrong side out is a sign of disappointment; to put it on and at once take it off is not good.

It has been said that if a widow looks in the full moon on any birthday, she will see her next husband.

It is a sure sign of a widow's marriage if she takes food at the house of a parson.

It is lucky to save some of your wedding cake.

It is unlucky for a maiden to marry in colors, or a widow in white.

It is unlucky to pick up an old glove or a piece of money; pass the first and spend the latter as quickly as you can.

Persons born in the same sign of the Zodiac will never be happy married.

It is a sure sign of disappointment if an unmarried person sit between a man and his wife at table.

It is said that if the crown of your head itch, you are going to be raised to some distinguished position.

If newly married people take a wedding trip on water, they should go up stream for luck, and not down.

For a widow to look into a tea or coffee pot is a sign of disappointment.

A woman who makes her own clothes will never be

rich. She should never make her wedding gown, nor put it on when finished until her wedding day.

When deeply depressed in spirits, good news is on the way; it is a sure sign.

A pair of scissors under your pillow will keep away bad dreams.

It is a sign of disappointment for a window blind to roll up askew.

If you drop food at table, it signifies some person is begrudging it to you.

Put a handful of salt in the fire when worried; it will relieve you.

Cut your nails on Monday, cut them for health.

Cut them on Tuesday, cut them for wealth.

Cut them on Wednesday, you will have news.

Cut them on Thursday, you will get new shoes.

Cut them on Friday, cut them for sorrow.

Cut them on Saturday, see your lover tomorrow.

The man or woman is sure to fail, who on Sunday cut their nails.

When a lath falls out of a bed, riches are coming.

Never tell a dream until your fast is broken.

When matches will go out, you are sure to have a disappointment.

When at sea a vessel is becalmed, wind can be produced by throwing a cat overboard, but he who does this thing will not reach shore alive.

A lighted lamp should be held in your right hand if you want luck.

Snow falling in the summer, or thunder in winter, indicates calamities and trouble of some kind.

If a person upsets his chair when rising from the table, be sure that he has been telling lies, for such is an old and proven saying.

Never stay long in a house you are visiting if you hear a clock strike at the wrong time.

If a pillow falls from a wedding bed, the one using it will die first.

A man who mends his own shoes will never be rich.

If you clean house on Sunday, hard work and small pay will be your lot the rest of the week.

It is considered unlucky to open and raise an umbrella in the house.

When the lid of your stove falls on the floor, you are likely to be the subject of undeserved scandal.

The new moon and the full moon are good times to transact important business or to marry.

It is bad luck for two persons to pass on the stairs. There is certain disappointment ahead.

It is considered unfortunate to sweep out a house which you are leaving.

If you lose your door key when away from home, it signifies you are wanted there.

A child with frequently dirty hands will grow up possessing riches.

If a glass falls in your presence and does not break, a journey or some pleasant surprise awaits you.

If you drop a comb, some disappointment may be yours; if

you step upon it before picking it up, it will prevent any misfortune.

If a pair of scissors drop and the point stick in the floor, more work is coming.

If you light a lamp and start to carry it somewhere and it goes out, it signifies you will be disappointed.

It is unlucky to rise from a table and light a lamp or candle for the purpose of finishing a meal.

It is good for the head of the family to take a slip or root of a plant or vine when removing to a new residence.

Never lay an umbrella on the bed. It is a sure sign of a quarrel.

To let an ironing board fall will bring you large numbers of visitors.

If you wish to own a house, learn to shut doors after you have passed between the posts.

The first pea pod a maiden finds in the spring, with nine peas in, before disturbing them, she should hang the pod over the door. If the first person to enter the house be a male, she will marry during the year. If a female, she will not.

If you forget to lock the door at night, you will hear of a death that concerns you.

Making tea too strong is a sign that you will make friends early.

Pie dough should be pinched off. The maker who cuts it will remain poor.

She who splits a clothes pin when hanging out clothes will soon hear bad news.

A fortunate journey is foretold if a torn napkin is handed you at the table.

To hang a garment on the door-knob is bad luck.

They who throw water out of the window will weep very soon.

It is a sign of company to accidentally place a kettle on the stove with the spout towards the back.

If a whisk broom falls from the hand of a negro when he brushes your clothes, it is a sure indication of a fight if you go out that evening.

A live coal flying out of the fire is a sure sign of wealth to the one it comes nearest.

It is a sign of a wedding for many tin pans to fall down at once.

To spit on the hands or on the first money you receive on a Monday is very lucky.

To change the date of a wedding is very unfortunate.

To throw an old shoe after the bride on her way to church is lucky.

To wear a bride's garter is a sure sign of marriage.

If a maid put a piece of bride cake which has been passed through the ring of the bride, under her pillow and sleep on that three nights, the third night she will see her future husband; if she dream only of women she will never be married.

Many icicles hanging from your house are a sign of wealth.

If the lock and door key persist in getting rusty, some friend is laying up money for you.

If a corpse does not get rigid for some time after

death, it is a sure indication that some one else in the family will die before the year is out.

When you take a pie out of the oven and it accidentally falls on the floor upside down, it indicates some one has died and left you a large amount of money.

If a door is pushed twice before it closes, another person will soon pass through that way.

To spill pepper is a sign of fighting.

A person sprinkled with pigeon's blood will die a violent death.

If you make your tea too weak, your friends will for--sake you.

They who wash on Monday have all the week to dry.
They who wash on Tuseday are not so awry.
They who wash on Wednesday are not so much to blame.
But they who wash on Thursday, wash for shame.
They who wash on Friday, wash in need.
But they who wash on Saturday, are sluts indeed.